Prison Journals
French Rev

duchesse de Louise Henriette Charlotte Philippine de
Durfort Duras, (Translator: Martha Ward Carey)

Alpha Editions

This edition published in 2024

ISBN 9789362519733

Design and Setting By
Alpha Editions
www.alphaedis.com
Email - info@alphaedis.com

Contents

PRISON LIFE DURING THE FRENCH REVOLUTION.

I was put under arrest, together with my father and mother, on August 23, 1793, at our château of Mouchy-le-Châtel, in the Department of the Oise. I was taken to the prison at Saint-François à Beauvais, in the old convent, on the 6th of October of the same year and to that at Chantilly on the 20th of the same month. There I remained until the 5th of April, 1794, when I was transferred to Paris, to the Collège du Plessis, from which I was liberated on the 19th of the following October.

WRITTEN IN 1801, THE YEAR IX. OF THE REPUBLIC.

The period of my confinement in different prisons during the Reign of Terror was so harassing that the idea of writing out its details did not then occur to me; but when I had the consolation of seeing my son once more, he was desirous of learning all about it. I feared that I should be overcome by my feelings if I tried to relate the details to him, and consequently determined to write the following memoirs.

My parents retired to their estate of Mouchy-le-Châtel, in the Department of the Oise, in the month of September, 1792. I accompanied them thither, and was their sole companion. They resolved, from prudential motives, to receive visits from no one. This privation cost my father nothing, for he was naturally shy, though the positions he had occupied had forced him to live constantly in the great world. My mother, who loved him dearly, accustomed herself to retirement with submission to the will of Providence, with the naturally happy disposition maintained through all the events of her life.

She loved system in all things, and she introduced it so successfully into our daily life that it passed rapidly. Reading, work, play, and walking filled up every moment. My parents took pleasure in furnishing refreshment to the harvesters during their weary labour, in sympathizing with their troubles, and in helping them by kindnesses. In spite of the position in which the Revolution placed my father, and the natural repugnance which he declared he felt for those who were engaged in it, he gave volunteers the means of paying their way. My father had, if I may so express myself, a passion for charity. His hands were always ready to bestow, and whenever he received a sum of money he would in a few hours declare, with satisfaction, that he had none of it left.

He could keep nothing when he knew that others were suffering; hospital visiting, aid rendered in private, all sorts of kind deeds and comforting words,—in fact all good works were familiar to him; in these alone he found happiness.

I have seen him refuse things which he might have considered necessary for himself in order to add to the number of his charities. Yet my father was born with a very unhappy disposition; the fortune, the honours, and all the pleasures that his position secured him were spoiled by the most miserable discontent. I frequently endeavoured, firmly and respectfully, to show him that Heaven had bestowed every gift upon him, and that nothing was wanting to his position. He listened patiently to what I had to say; but I did not succeed in convincing him. I worried myself and gained nothing. My mother, on the contrary, often said to me that if she should return to society she would not desire to change her manner of living in the least. She had a charmingly happy disposition, and was never out of humour for a moment.

Several times during the Revolution it was proposed that I should emigrate. One of my relatives sent for me at different periods, and urged me to consent to do so. I always refused, having a great repugnance to leaving my country, and desiring to watch over the old age of my parents, who were already separated from some of their children.

How great would have been my regret had I not remained with them up to the moment when I was deprived of my liberty. I shall retain to my latest breath the memory of their kindness, and the tenderest gratitude for the good example and daily lessons in virtue which I received from them.

But to return to the details of our family life at Mouchy. Every day I was filled with wonder to see my father, who from his youth had been accustomed to command (he had at the age of seven been given the reversion of the governorship of Versailles, after his father's death), obey without complaint the Revolutionary laws and all those who executed them. Everything worried him under the old régime, yet during the Reign of Terror he was calm because he was entirely resigned to the will of God. Religion had regulated all the actions of his life. It was really, for him, eternal happiness.

We suffered great anxiety during our sojourn at Mouchy. We were utterly ignorant of the fate of my elder brother.[1] A price had been put on his head and the notice of it posted at the corners of the streets of Paris, and the newspapers had stated that he had been guillotined. One afternoon, in the month of October (the 10th), we saw approaching us quite a large body of troops composed of Hussars and National Guards from different villages of the estate of Mouchy. It was preceded by a commissioner of the Committee of General Security, named Landry, who came to arrest my brother, believing that he was concealed in the castle. We were surprised, but not frightened. It was absurd to suppose that he would have chosen his own father's house for his hiding-place. They searched everywhere under pretext of taking him and of seizing arms, but they found nothing.

The official report made by the commissioner and the municipality proves this.

The drawing up of the report and the search lasted from five o'clock in the evening to eleven. Landry, called upon my father to denounce his son, though he could not even know whether he was alive or not. He answered with much dignity that such a demand was as harsh as it was unusual, and that he would not accede to it; yet he asked Landry, to take something to eat, and lent him one of his saddle horses to take him back to his carriage. My father, who was naturally very fiery, knew how to control himself when the importance of the occasion required it.

The officer of the Hussars who commanded the detachment was a very excellent man. He told us that he was marching with his troop along the highway from Beauvais, to Paris; that being required by the commissioner of the Committee of General Security to accompany him to Mouchy, he had been obliged to obey him, though with great repugnance, and that he came with the kindest intentions possible. He gave me an immediate proof of this; for he whispered in my ear that if my brother was in the house he would advise me to hasten his escape, and that he would be very glad of it. I have retained a feeling of real gratitude for this officer, whose name I do not know; he was from the region of Rouen.

The intense animosity which was shown in the attempt to capture my brother increased our anxiety concerning our own fate. A report, circulated by the newspapers, that he was in England somewhat allayed our anxiety; and Monsieur Noël (my father's man of business, who has given proof of the strongest attachment to our family) afterward assured us of its truth. When he entered the drawing-room we were much agitated, not knowing what news he was about to announce to us.

Various accounts have been given of the manner in which my brother escaped the scaffold. Some have said that he escaped from prison by the payment of a hundred thousand crowns to Manuel, then Procureur, of the Commune; others, that he left Paris disguised as a wagoner, and had been seen passing along several roads.

The truth is that he was never arrested, and that he found good and brave men who were kind enough to hide him in their houses; that he remained for several hours in the very top of the Louvre, stretched upon a beam, at the very moment when the famous search of September, 1792, was made; and that afterward he escaped by means of a passport to Granville, where Monsieur Mauduit, his son's old tutor, a naval commissioner, assisted him to embark for Dover.

Monsieur Mauduit, was guillotined, but he made no mention of my brother's affairs at his trial. My poor brother, having sailed from port, thought he had escaped death. A storm compelled his vessel to return to the port. He was obliged to hide himself in a place so close that his suffering for want of air came near causing him to betray himself. The search ended just in time to save his life, and he again set sail. It is also false that he used large sums of money to get out of his danger. He was not forced to spend more than two thousand crowns. The knowledge that he was out of danger diminished our daily increasing anxiety.

We had peaceful consciences, but the condition of affairs was becoming very threatening, and the future very disturbing. We often talked it over. I had the comfort of alleviating the situation of my dear parents, and they showed great pleasure in receiving my attentions. I concealed from them the terrible thoughts which constantly came to my mind, and occupied myself in distracting them from those by which they were sometimes agitated. We had not even the consolation of religious worship, the curate of the parish having taken the oath to the civil constitution exacted from the clergy; but we had had until our arrest opportunity to hear Mass from a Catholic priest. I prayed to God with all my heart for grace sufficient to endure all the terrible things that I foresaw in our future experience. About the 15th of August, 1793, Collot d'Herbois, and Isoré were sent *en mission* into the Departments of the Aisne and the Oise. They immediately put into execution there the decree regarding suspects, though this was not done in Paris until the 18th of the following September. Consequently all the priests and nobles were arrested. On the 23d of August the municipality of Mouchy, notified us of the order to remain under arrest in our residences until the houses of confinement were ready to receive us. The mayor, who was a zealous patriot, disposed to enforce an extreme rather than a moderate execution of the severe laws, told us that this was a measure for the public safety,—a phrase much in use during the Reign of Terror,—and that we need not be alarmed. We were allowed a space of a hundred paces in the park to walk in, and the free use of the courtyard, provided the grating was closed. We went there sometimes to talk with the people. This way of living was only an apprenticeship to the slavery that was impending. One quite singular fact was that, the population of Mouchy, being small, our own dependents acted National Guardsmen, and stood sentinel at our gates. I suppose there were those among them who took pleasure in doing this; for charity's sake I pass over their conduct in silence.

A very few of them, however, gave my parents strong proof of their attachment. I will give a list of their names at the end of these memoirs.

The municipality of Mouchy, sent a petition to the Department of the Oise, asking to be allowed to keep us within its limits and on its own responsibility. It referred in kindly terms to our wise and prudent conduct, and to our submission to the laws. The Department of the Oise, acceded to the petition relative to my parents; but they did not consider me old enough, and it had been said at Beauvais, that they wished to have a titled woman at Chantilly. Consequently a sergeant of the national gendarmes came with four horsemen to take me to Beauvais. I was at that moment sick in bed. The village surgeon, named Marais, and my father's physician considered that I was in no condition to be moved; but their attestations were not sufficient, and the sergeant sent for the physician of the Department, who decided that it was necessary for me to remain at Mouchy, and drew up an official paper in regard to my condition. I remained about five weeks to recuperate, during which time several petitions were sent to the Department in my favour. Monsieur Legendre went to see Collot d'Herbois, and Isoré. But all these efforts were fruitless.

I was so fully persuaded that I was going to be incarcerated that I packed up all my belongings, and hoped that my punishment would suffice for all. It cost me great suffering to leave my honoured parents to whom I had the comfort of being useful.

I was a little better, and had been for a few days going down into the courtyard to take the air, when I saw a man arrive dressed in the uniform of the National Guard,—he was the commander of the Guard at Beauvais, and his name was Poulain. I immediately suspected with what mission he was charged, and arranged with him that my parents should not know of the time of my departure. We agreed that at a signal which he would give me I should under some pretext leave the drawing-room and not return to it. It was important that my parents should not undergo too much emotion. I went up to them quietly and told them of my arrest. At first they bore the announcement bravely. I avoided saying anything to them which could agitate them, and conversed with the officer upon ordinary subjects. He searched neither my packages nor my papers. At last the moment came when I was obliged to leave them.

I seemed to foresee that I should never again behold my parents.

I went away, saying nothing, but feeling broken-hearted. I felt as though my limbs were giving way under me. And that scene of grief, which I am describing on the very spot where it took place, still causes me deep emotion as I recall it; but there are feelings which it is impossible to express. I have been told since, and Madame Latour also relates it in her journal, that my father and mother remained in a frightful state of dejection; they would take no nourishment, and passed the nights weeping and constantly reiterating that they had been deprived of half their existence when their dear daughter was taken away.

It was on the 6th of October, 1793, that I left Mouchy, at five o'clock in the evening, in one of my father's carriages, with Monsieur Poulain and my maid. We reached Beauvais, after a drive of two hours. The carriage tilted as we drove along; the officer endeavoured to assure me there was no danger. I somewhat insolently replied, 'I fear God, dear Abner, and have no other fear.'[2]

I was, however, suffering intensely inwardly. Fortunately the darkness concealed the tears that fell from my eyes. I prayed Heaven earnestly to sustain my courage.

The officer had orders to have me alight at the prison. He went to the Revolutionary committee to ask permission for me to spend the night at his house; it was granted him. I learned afterward that this kind act, done without my knowledge, and the irreproachable manner in which he had treated me had brought persecution upon him, and that he had been obliged to flee from Beauvais. His wife received me very politely. She tried to make me take some supper; I accepted a very little, but it may easily be imagined that my appetite was not of the best. I passed a wretched night. The desolate situation of my parents weighed constantly upon my mind and heart,—their age, their loneliness (they who so short a time before had been surrounded by so many relatives and friends), and the uncertainty of their future, which left so much to be feared.

I did not have the grief of awakening, so terrible to the unhappy. I received all sorts of care from my kind hostess, who had me breakfast with her husband and herself. After that I set out for a convent of nuns of the third order of Saint Francis, which was occupied by some sick soldiers, and by prisoners who were placed here temporarily until a sufficient number were collected to form a convoy and be sent to Chantilly. I entered a drawing-room where the company was assembled; it was composed of ecclesiastics, a few nobles, and some women. The most important ones were, among others, a man named Poter, head of the manufactory of Chantilly, a nun, a sutler, etc. They scrutinized my countenance. I took pains to please my new companions, and then asked to be conducted to my lodging-room, which was a former linen closet, far away from every one, so that if I had wanted anything it would have been impossible for me to make myself heard.

Monsieur Allou, our neighbour from Mouchy, who frequently came to see my parents, rendered me all the service in his power, and persuaded me to have a young girl, a prisoner, sleep in my apartment. I agreed, though with extreme reluctance, for I greatly preferred being alone. Sad thoughts prevented my sleeping, besides my being so unaccustomed to lying upon sacking for a bed. I at once had to give up the habit of having a light, upon which I was very dependent; but being destined to undergo great privations, I from that moment renounced the conveniences of life and set myself to learn how to attend to my own wants. As a beginning, I made some chocolate, which was horrible. Seeing my incapacity, I took some lessons, and after a day or two I ventured to invite one of my neighbours to breakfast; and she felt herself obliged, for politeness' sake, to praise my new talent. I arranged my employments so that the days might not seem so long. I read, I wrote, and I fixed a certain time to walk in the cloisters. They were always filled with the odour of sulphur, which was much used in the house for treating the soldiers afflicted with the itch. The air was not good on account of the gutters of stagnant water which crossed the yard. We were not allowed to go into the garden; it was appropriated to the use of the convalescents. The old chapel of the nuns was still in existence, and most of the prisoners went there to say their prayers. I sometimes thought how great in the eyes of Heaven must be the difference between us and the pure spirits who had gone there before us. They had voluntarily given up their liberty to consecrate it to God, while I felt that the loss of mine was a great sacrifice. Formerly the walls of this sacred place echoed only the praises of God, and now within them the soldiers blasphemed undisturbed. One day while I was at confession I was deafened by the songs of the Terror, the guardhouse of the Revolutionary army being just back of my room.

Among the prisoners there were some venerable priests, who set us an example of perfect submission to the will of Providence. I tried hard to imitate them. Shortly after my arrival at St. François the steward of Mouchy, named Legendre (whom I shall set down at the end of these memoirs among those persons who have been most devoted to us), was arrested and thrown into our prison on account of his attachment to my parents. I was particularly distressed at this, because if I had sent warning to him at Beauvais, when Monsieur Poulain came to arrest me at Mouchy, he would have had time to escape. I told him all I felt on this point. I shall have occasion to speak of him again more than once.

Upon a petition from Monsieur Poulain to the Revolutionary committee of Beauvais, my waiting-woman (Mademoiselle Dubois) was granted permission to come for an hour each day to St. François, to assist me in making my toilet. To that I have never attached the slightest importance; but it was a real satisfaction to me to receive through her some tidings from my parents, and to send them information concerning myself, and which they too received with kindest interest. Imagine how terrible a shock it was to me when I heard through Monsieur Allou, our neighbour from Mouchy, that they had been carried off on the 16th of October, by order of the Committee of General Security and taken to Paris to the great prison of La Force. I knew none of the details (they are recounted in Madame Latour's memoirs), and was completely overwhelmed. This poor man was moved also, and we wept together. I had hoped that the advanced age of my parents, their virtues, and the voice of the poor would appease the anger of the established authorities; but Robespierre, having learned that the great proprietors who had estates in the environs, had retired to them, and were living quietly upon them, resolved to drive them away and have them put in prison.

My parents passed only twenty-four hours in La Force. They were transferred to the Luxembourg, which they left only to pass into eternity.

Every day I heard sad news through prisoners who read the public papers, and who desired to communicate it to me. I refused to listen, thinking that to do so was only to incur additional pain. One day, when I was wondering what my parents were undergoing, I saw enter the cloister Monsieur d'Aryon, a captain of the National Guard (a very honest man, to whom I was afterward under many obligations), who seemed anxious not to meet me, so entirely was he dismayed by his mission. He sent a prisoner to deliver to me my order of imprisonment, of which the following is a copy:—

BEAUVAIS, this 19th of October,

28th day of the 2d month of

the year II. of the Republic.

You are informed that you are to start for Chantilly on the night of this day, Saturday to Sunday. You would do well to make all your preparations to take with you everything absolutely necessary to you.

If you have occasion to procure a carriage, let me know.

(Signed)

E. PORTIER. MICHEL,

TAQUET, DUFOUR,

Procureur, of the Commune.

To Madame Duras [la dame Duras], whose carriage is at the Golden Lion. She can use it if she wishes to do so.

It was addressed to 'Madame Duras, St. François.'

As soon as we had been informed of the order to leave, we became anxious to know whether all the prisoners at St. François were to be of the party. Only a portion of them were destined at that time for Chantilly. We passed the whole day in packing our belongings. Mine were taken there from Mouchy, which spared me for that time the worry of moving them, to which I was afterward compelled to accustom myself. I forgot to say that the keeper of St. François was the most humane of all under whom I was placed. I could not determine whether I was sorry or glad to change my prison. Those to which I was going were infinitely more wretched; but I did not then know their terrible methods.

About eleven o'clock at night we were told to get into the carriage, but the train did not start till midnight. It was composed of wagons and carriages of different sorts. I took in mine Monsieur de Reignac, an officer of the King's Constitutional Guard, who was afterward guillotined, a nun from the Hôtel-Dieu at Beauvais, and my waiting-woman. My coachman, to whom this journey was exceedingly distressing, wept the whole way. We were escorted by the Beauvais, National Guard, part on foot and part on horseback. As it was moonlight the people came out in front of their doors to hoot at us and throw stones at us. The train which had preceded us had been insulted infinitely worse. Monsieur Descourtils, an old and very estimable soldier, who had on all occasions rendered services to the town of Beauvais, and also Monsieur Wallon, the kind patron of the poor, were treated in the most outrageous manner.

Our procession moved so slowly, and we stopped so often, that we did not reach Clermont until eleven o'clock in the morning, after having come six leagues. My nun, who was not accustomed to travelling in a carriage, was almost nauseated all the way. I read throughout almost the whole journey.

We dined at an inn in Clermont. The people watched us dismount with an expression of pity. This feeling, which it is generally so undesirable to inspire, gave us pleasure on account of its rarity during the Reign of Terror. Nothing worthy of remark took place during our short stay at Clermont, unless it was the manner in which we were guarded. Our escort, being obliged to rest and get something to eat, confided us to the care of the National Guard of the city, among whom there were some prisoners who had been placed there to increase the size of the troop. The vicinity of Fitz-James made me sadly recall memories of the past. I had been so happy there from my earliest childhood; now nothing was left me but to regret it; all those with whom I had spent my life there were either dead or gone away. But while I was giving way to these sad thoughts, we were told it was time to leave. The train started, and we reached Chantilly at three o'clock.

It would be difficult to describe the confusion caused by the unpacking of the many vehicles loaded with mattresses and other things belonging to the prisoners, all thrown haphazard in the court, without other order than to unload them, and that the bundles should not be taken upstairs till the next day, when there would be time to examine them.

Consequently it was the custom to go to bed on a chair the first night, after a very scanty supper, or to accept the mattress of some prisoner willing to deprive himself of it. As we passed the iron grating at the entrance of the place, I recalled the 2d of September, and said to Monsieur de Reignac that it was quite probable that we were being gathered together to be made to submit to the same fate; he seemed to think so too. Several attempts had been made to invent conspiracies, which had in fact no real existence at Chantilly any more than in other prisons. In order to render the name prison less terrible, they were called houses of arrest, of justice, of detention, etc.; but as during the Reign of Terror these words were synonyms, I shall make use of them without distinction. The whole party was taken into a beautifully gilded chapel, where I had heard Mass in the time of the Prince de Condé. It was quite filled with bags of flour; I found one which was placed in a comfortable position, and seated myself on it. Then the steward of the house, by name Notté, member for the Department of the Oise, mounted on the altar steps to call the roll, holding in his hand the list of those who composed the party; he had on his right a man named Marchand (who was the son of a very respectable waiting-woman of my aunt, Madame la Maréchale de Noailles), an agent of the Revolutionary army, who was in the confidence of the Committee of Public Safety. He seemed to take pleasure, as the names of the priests and nobles were called, in saying the harshest and most cutting things to them. A village vicar from the environs of Beauvais, and I had the worst of it all. This poor priest was quite in a tremor; but as for me, I did not mind it at all. This man Marchand asked Notté if he had taken care to see that I was very poorly lodged, and he replied that he had selected for me the smallest room to be had. When the roll-call was over, Mademoiselle Dubois, my waiting-woman, asked permission to remain in prison with me. The commissioners refused her request, and declared their determination of sending away all those not prisoners who up to that time had remained in the place. She was much grieved at parting from me. I was not sorry to give her up, for I had been extremely worried to see her suffering and deprived of liberty on account of her attachment to me. I remember with gratitude the feeling she showed for me at that time, and I am very glad to record it in this memoir. After a very long and wearisome discussion we left the chapel, quite curious to see our new quarters. I was agreeably surprised when they conducted me to a small room, neat and prettily gilded, where I was to be alone. Notté had had the good manners to keep it for me. I valued it the more when I saw the lodgings of my travelling companions. Several prisoners came to see me. I was not acquainted with one of them. I seemed to have been shipwrecked on an island inhabited by good people. They welcomed me heartily, and I was permitted to have my belongings, which had come from Mouchy, sent up to me at once. Consequently I had the pleasure of sleeping on a bed,—a rare thing on the day of one's arrival. Several of my neighbours were kind enough to help me make it up. I was quite overcome, and terribly fatigued. I received all these kindnesses as graciously as possible, but was impatient to be left to repose. Mademoiselle de Pons, now Madame de Tourzel, came with a message from her mother, asking me to supper; and Madame de Chevigné invited me to breakfast next morning. I accepted the second invitation with pleasure. I had never known these ladies intimately. They were the only ones belonging to the court who were in the house. I had only met them at the houses of my acquaintances.

The fatigue I had undergone the day before made me sleep. I had scarcely risen when Mademoiselle Lèfvre, the sister-in-law of the steward of Mouchy, came to my room to give me information concerning the inhabitants of our prison, and advice about my own arrangements,—all of which was very useful to me. It is a very sad thing to find oneself utterly alone in the midst of a crowd. Monsieur Notté paid me a visit; I did not find his face so severe as it had seemed on the arrival of our party, when he stood beside the commissioner of the Revolutionary army. He spoke pleasantly to me, and told me that, as the prisoners were very much crowded in their lodgings, he thought it best to put some one with me in a little cabinet which was under my control. In order to enter it one had to pass through my room. He allowed me to select the person, and I chose the hospital sister who had come from Beauvais, with me. She was a good woman, the daughter of a village farrier, without education, but a great help to me in the daily needs of life. I had an opportunity to show her my gratitude for it all during a severe illness of hers, when I acted not only as her nurse, but also as her physician, as she was not willing to see a doctor. She frequently gave me proof of the fact that when one has not received certain ideas in youth it is impossible to comprehend some of the simplest things. I would alter my phrases in every possible way in order to enable her to understand what I meant,—among other things respect for opinion, etc. She remained with me until I was removed to Paris, and was never annoying to me. This was a great blessing, since our companionship was enforced. I soon began to pay visits among our colony, which was composed of very incongruous material. There were priests, nobles, nuns, magistrates, soldiers, merchants, and a large number of what were called 'sans-culottes,' from all parts of the country, and who were excellent people. I had near me a mail-carrier, a barmaid, and other domestics, whom I highly esteemed. They had become greatly attached to a venerable curate from Beauvais who lodged with them. They called him their father, rendered him many services, and took perfect care of him during a serious illness which he had while in prison. I first learned something of the character and habits of our companions, and which of them seemed most honest. They told me that we had among us samples of all sorts of persons and opinions. There were priests, real confessors of Jesus Christ, to be revered on account of their patience and their charity, others who had renounced their profession, and declared from the pulpit that they had formerly only uttered fables. One of these unprincipled priests, a man still very young, who had served in a regiment, often said that he did not know why he was kept in prison, for on every occasion since the Revolution he had done whatever he had been desired to do. When civic festivals were given in the village of Chantilly he had been the composer of couplets. He wore habitually the national uniform. We had two abbesses,—the abbess of the Parc-aux-Dames and the abbess of Royal-Lieu, Madame de Soulanges, who was nearly eighty years old, and had been under-governess to Madame Louise at Fontevrault, and was tenderly beloved by her. During her sojourns in Compèigne the princess used to go to see her every day. (Madame Louise, daughter of Louis XV., a Carmelite at St. Denis, had been brought up at the abbey of Fontevrault, together with Madame Victoire and Madame Sophie.)

I discovered, soon after my arrival at Chantilly that loss of liberty unites neither minds nor hearts, and that people are the same in prison as in the world at large,—jealous, intriguing, false; for there were among us many spies,—an epithet, however, which was often lightly bestowed. I endeavoured to be polite to every one, and intimate only with a very small circle.

I made some visits every day, and received visitors after dinner, during which time I also worked. Sometimes some patriots whom I recognized quite well, pretended to be aristocrats, so as to make me talk; it was without doubt the most disagreeable part of the day. The time passed without great weariness, for I filled it up with prayer and reading, and a little walking in a courtyard, walled on four sides, and very dreary looking. At first we were able to go to the grating and talk with persons outside; but it was not desired that we should do this, and to prevent it planks were placed over the grating. These concealed the outer view and made communication impossible. On the third story there were terraces on the leads, upon which all our windows opened; and these windows, in several instances, also served as doors; only one person could pass through them at a time. It was really a comical sight, this file of prisoners, dressed in all sorts of costumes, and going around and around like a panorama. We were frequently obliged to stop on account of the great number of promenaders. Mademoiselle de Pons, who played on the piano, accompanied on the violin by Monsieur de Corberon (an officer of the French Guards, who was afterwards guillotined), entertained us most agreeably; she occupied one of the apartments of which I have just spoken. The view from it was very pleasant,—the most beautiful rippling waters, numerous villages, a superb forest, fine buildings belonging to the château, and a green lawn most charming to look upon. I thoroughly examined every portion of our prison. Several of the large rooms had been divided by plank partitions which were only six or seven feet high. Those who occupied these compartments during the winter suffered excessively from cold. In the rooms which were not so divided there were put as many as twenty-five persons. I noticed the arrangement of one of these communities, in which the curtain-less beds were placed so close together that during the day the prisoners, in order to move around, were obliged to pile them up on top of one another. Here is a list of the individuals occupying this room: A republican general and his wife, a curate from Noyon, twenty-seven years old, several young men, two estimable mothers of families, with five or six daughters from fourteen to twenty years. In another there were a soldier with two or three nuns. The one next to mine contained a general, called Monsieur de Coincy, eighty-three years old, who still retained his strength, his wife, his son, his daughter, a nun of the Visitation, and Mesdemoiselles de Grammont-Caderousse, the eldest of whom was about fourteen. A special annoyance in our prison was the mingling of the sexes in the same lodging. I was the more thankful for my little cell. Marchand, the commissioner of the Revolutionary army, came to make me a visit; he found nothing to complain of in the furnishing of my apartment, which was composed of a servant's bed, two chairs, and a table. The beds and the trunks served as seats when the company was too numerous. Generally luxury was an offence to him. I told him he could find no fault with mine. I was mistaken; he answered that I as well as my parents had once had too much of it. He went from one end to the other of the place, and took it into his head, in order to annoy those ladies who seemed somewhat careful of their toilets, to order them to have their hair cut off; and he also sent *sans-culottes* to sleep in their rooms. These poor fellows were as much worried at this as those who were compelled to submit to it. They used to come as late as they possibly could and go away very early in the morning. They were very well behaved, with the exception of a cobbler from Compiègne, of whom his hosts complained bitterly; he was ill-tempered and annoying. One of his comrades, probably better reared, came near dying of colic through his politeness in not wishing to awaken those with whom he was forced to lodge.

Care had been taken, in order to avoid too active a correspondence between the prisoners and outsiders, to send those who were inhabitants of the district of Senlis to the abbey of St. Paul at Beauvais, and those of Beauvais, to Chantilly. We could not write even to our parents, nor could we receive news from them without a great deal of trouble. Of all the privations we were forced to undergo, this was the hardest to bear. While Notté was at the head of the house, the prisoners continually complained of him, though our situation was endurable. The wretched are naturally fault-finding.

I assured them that if he went away it would be worse for us; and so it actually happened. This man was passionate but not wicked. I had found out that one should never ask him anything in the presence of other persons, because he feared lest they might be indiscreet; but in private he was quite accommodating. I never had any reason to complain of him. By one of the strange chances of the Revolution, he is now in want, and at the very time when I am writing this memoir, is soliciting my protection, which I would willingly grant him if it were better worth having.

I was generally strictly obedient to the rules of the household, and consequently had to endure fewer annoyances than those who strove to evade them. It is true that they changed so frequently that it was difficult to keep the run of them.

We were guarded at first by the gendarmerie, afterward by the National Guard of Chantilly. I was informed of this by a carpenter who, while doing some work in my room, told me he was now our military commander. I found it necessary to ask his permission to do something the next day, and I did so in such a serious manner that Madame Séguier, who was present, could not help laughing.

The Revolutionary army succeeded the National Guard, and made its entrance into the house in a manner suitable to the functions with which it was charged. At ten o'clock in the evening we learned that there were cannon pointed toward the château, and at the same moment we heard the grating open amid songs which sounded more like rage than joy. The vanguard was preceded by cannon, drums, and torches. Women mingled with the procession. The refrain of 'Ça ira, les aristocrates à la lanterne!' was repeated with stubborn animosity. My neighbours were seized with terror, and rushed trembling into my apartment. I reassured them as well as I could without knowing why, except that the feeling of fear is one to which I do not readily yield.

When the troop had finished its dances and songs in the courtyard, and gone through a sort of march, it placed its sentinels and retired. I had the full benefit of the performance, as my windows opened on the courtyard.

I cannot now remember the exact time, but a few days after the scene I have just described took place, several prisoners were sent to the prisons at Paris, among them Monsieur de Vernon, Master of Horse to the king, who had gout in his hands, but on whom they put handcuffs. A curate named Daniel was sent off with him. They were taken to the prison of the Carmelites on the Rue de Vaugirard. A party of thirty persons followed them immediately. Madame de Pontevès seeing them carrying off her husband, asked a commissioner named Martin for permission to go with him. He answered her roughly, granted her request, and then separated them when they reached Paris. One of them was put in the Madelonnettes, and the other in Ste. Pélagie. In order to fill the prisons of Paris it was sometimes necessary to draw recruits from the neighbouring prisons; for this purpose different pretexts were made. Evil designs were imputed to the prisoners,—such as anti-revolutionary projects; for instance, one was called an agitator if he spoke to the keeper or to the commissioner in order to make known his wants.

When any one came to inspect us I kept in the background. I was obliged, however, to appear before Martin, the commissioner extraordinary, who was accompanied by a man with a red cap, and had a roll-call of all the prisoners. He only asked me my name. A sort of officer who was with them said that he had dined once at the house of Monsieur de Duras, at Bordeaux, and had been very well entertained. I did not continue the conversation. Some of the prisoners pleaded their causes, and petitioned to be allowed to go free. I withdrew as soon as I possibly could.

Monsieur de Saint-Souplet, the king's esquire, who was constantly worrying about getting the news, was taken away, arraigned before the Revolutionary tribunal, and perished on the scaffold with his father, who was eighty years old, and one of his brothers. He was denounced by one of his servants; but the latter was guillotined with him for not having betrayed his master sooner. We now began to hear of a great many executions; that of Madame de Larochefoucauld-Durtal caused me intense sorrow, and also made me extremely anxious for the future. She was a widow of thirty years, lived a most retired life, caring for her parents, and occupied solely with their happiness and with works of charity. She was carried off from the Anglaises, where she had been imprisoned with her mother, who was very old and extremely infirm. She was taken before the Revolutionary tribunal as a witness for her uncle, Monsieur de l'Aigle, whose mind was affected. He compromised her in consequence of his weakness of mind, and the address of a letter which did not belong to her was made a pretext to remove her from the position of witness to that of criminal. Sentence was passed at once upon her. As something was the matter with the guillotine that day, she spent twenty-four hours in the record-office awaiting her execution; during this time she lovingly and zealously exhorted her uncle to meet death bravely. She assured him many times that she forgave him for being the cause of her own death; and after having somewhat aroused his senses, she showed him how to die resignedly.

I could not understand how it was that the prisoners who were every day hearing sad news should feel the need of being amused. They assembled to play with high stakes, have music, dance, etc. A Monsieur Leloir, an architect from Paris, and quite facetious, was the leader of all the amusements. I was constantly invited to join them, but always refused.

Notté was sent away from the place, and a grocer from Chantilly, named Vion, became our keeper. This was the golden age of our house. Leloir had influence over him, and as he was one of the prisoners, we reaped the benefit of it; but the commissioners of the Revolutionary committees of the neighbouring villages, the greater part of whom were employed about us, were able to persecute us. In fact, any one could do so who chose to take the trouble. I will give an example of this which is ludicrous enough: A man named Bizoti, employed as a wagoner, had the curiosity to pay us a visit, and took real pleasure in abusing all the priests. There was an old maid from Vandeuil, once fond of the chase, who was in the habit of wearing a costume somewhat masculine, composed of a man's hat and a dressing-gown. The wagoner-citizen said to her: 'I know you; you are a curate;' and then he addressed to her the same abusive language he had used to the priests. Loud bursts of laughter followed this. I sometimes went to see this spinster, who was very original.

I was very fond of the family of Monsieur de Boury, a captain of the French Guards, who had a wife and ten children. They are examples of every virtue; the father is truly religious, honourable, and well instructed; the wife is sweet and good. The harmony that pervades their life recalls that of the old Patriarchs. They were entirely resigned to the decrees of Providence, and preached to us by their example. A number of pious prisoners used to gather in their apartment for prayer and edifying reading. In all the house it was the spot I enjoyed most. It seemed to me that there one breathed purer air than anywhere else.

My chief amusement was to watch from my window the young people of fourteen or fifteen, who played foot-ball in the courtyard, forgetful of their captivity, and never dreaming that execution could await them. Alas! The Terror laid hold on one of them. Young Goussainville, only fifteen years old, was beheaded with his father. Several of the prisoners had brought their children with them, even nursing babies. (Madame de Maupeou was nursing one.) These children were of all ages; I could never understand how any one dared bring them into houses so full of dangers, to say nothing of the bad air. The laws now forbid persons to be received among the prisoners who desire to be there for the purpose of caring for those they love, which is very wise. We had at Chantilly several examples of that sort of devotion. The spirit of everything there was, in general, better than in the prison where I have since been.

Our keepers took a notion to put us at a common table, and this custom was afterward elegantly called 'eating in mess.' At first, during our sojourn at Chantilly, we were fed by eating-house keepers, established at the château. The keeper Désignon was one of the number. He served, beyond comparison, the worst fare to his customers; but I took it from motives of policy, knowing that he had more consideration for those whose food he furnished. He never failed in respect to me. Although he was only the subaltern of the commissioner, he arrogated the right to abuse those of the prisoners who asked to change their lodgings or to be less crowded together in the rooms they were occupying. The new arrangement was a calamity for him, since he had contracted with the government to supply all those who could not pay for their own food, and of these there was a large number.

A table was set in the gilded gallery of the Petit Château,[3] without a cloth, and with two hundred covers. The tables were reset three times, for there were many more than six hundred prisoners in the house; but the old and infirm were allowed to remain in their apartments. One of the tables was occupied by priests and unmarried men, the second by married people and children, the third by those who were alone; and this was my situation. The places were all numbered, and each of us had a duplicate number. When the bell rang, we came like children going to school, with baskets, in which were our plates, goblets, etc. Often the previous dinner was not over, and we had to stand a long time in groups in the drawing-room, which was next the gallery. We ate soup, which was only water with a few lentils such as are fed to horses, grass for spinach, sprouted potatoes, and a perfectly disgusting stew called *ratatouille*. I suppose that this word is not in the dictionary of the Academy, and that the Institute is not likely to put it there. We rose from the table hungry. There was a very hearty young man to whom we used to send all that was left at our table, in order to appease his hunger in some degree.

The members of the Revolutionary committee, with the officers of our guard, marched around our table with their red caps on their heads. There was one of them—the peruke-maker for the whole company—who watched us closely, to see if any one abstained from meat. Under such circumstances it was not easy to keep Lent. Many persons, however, did keep it strictly, although the grand vicars of the diocese had exempted three days.

Our tables were surrounded by sentinels of the Revolutionary army. I sometimes conversed with them. I found one among them to whom his service was extremely disagreeable. He was a servant whom want had compelled to take such a wretched position. He pitied us, and would willingly have afforded some alleviation of our terrible condition. One of the guards' duties was to accompany, with drawn sabres, the washerwomen when they came to bring and carry away our linen. This performance was truly humiliating, and I made some effort to avoid its most embarrassing details.

One day a commissioner delivered a most atrocious reproof to the keeper. He told him that there did not enough prisoners die in the house. In fact, through lack of care, the bad food, and the incapacity of the health officers, a great many would have died; but Providence protected them, and their constitutions held out much better than could have been expected.

One day as we were dining in the gallery of the Petit Château, I recalled the beautiful pictures which formerly adorned it, the armour of the great Condé, pierced with bullets, his victories represented by the great painters, all the festivals I had attended in that place; but happily these ideas came to me rarely. I generally had there very commonplace thoughts; those which concerned my bill of fare,—such as the endeavour to introduce into it, by means of bribery, a pound of butter or a few eggs,—absorbed me. In this connection I had a very amusing encounter with our new commissioner, named Perdrix. This man had a grotesque figure, and wore a costume not less so. His former profession had been to paint the dogs of Monsieur the Prince of Condé. He probably imagined it would add to his dignity to be more severe than his predecessors. We were allowed to speak to him only through an opening made in the wall. I one day presented myself at this strange parlour to ask him to allow me to have six pounds of chocolate which he had held back; he replied with dignity that he would allow me exactly as much of it as was good for my stomach. I assured him that in order to have the dose exact the only way was to have me breakfast every morning with the surgeon, and said moreover, that I wanted to give it to a sick man. He did not grant my request, and I went away somewhat angry at not being able to obtain the nourishment which kept up my strength. My charwoman, who fortunately was also his, brought back to me the full supply the next day.

I will leave off these small details, and tell how a poor soldier of the Revolutionary army, the father of a family, being unacquainted with Chantilly, arrived there in the night, and losing his way, fell into one of the moats which surrounded the castle. At daybreak some of the prisoners saw the man struggling and screaming. Monsieur de Bouquerolle, an officer of the navy, who knew how to swim (he was the eldest son of the much respected family of Boury), started to go into the water after him. The sentinel prevented his doing so, telling him that it was a prisoner who had escaped, and left the man to perish. His body was found afterward, and it was recognized as that of one of their own men. Monsieur de Corberon and a curate asked that the body should be brought into the house, in order to try the usual means of restoring the drowned to life. This was granted them; and they used every means in their power for several hours, but without success. After this act of cruelty one can imagine how incensed the prisoners were. Well, they had their revenge in taking up a collection for the widow and children which amounted to six hundred francs. These were the people who during the Revolution were called criminals.

The parties sent off increased in number to an alarming degree. Each day when one went off we were filled with consternation. Husbands were separated from their wives, mothers from their children; and those who had no interests so dear had to regret some one of their companions. We did not know where they were taken, nor what took place in the prisons at Paris. For my part, I imagined them to be still worse than ours; and I was quite right, in spite of the continual vexations, hunger, and daily anxieties which we experienced.

One evening as I was taking a walk on the terraces in the delightful moonlight, which gleamed over the forest and made the waters sparkle, my ears delighted by the rippling sound, my eyes taking in all the beauty which surrounded me, I congratulated myself upon being, after all, less unfortunate than a great many persons whom I loved and respected. The wretched situation of my parents came over me at that moment so terribly that I shed tears. I scarcely ever received news from them, or from any of the friends who were dear to me.

Eatables were forbidden to be brought to us, lest letters should be concealed in them; and this reduced us sometimes to the necessity of eating soup made of salt and water only.

The Revolutionary guard took it into their heads to go on patrol from ten to eleven o'clock in the evening. They put out the lights, and made the prisoners go to bed. One day the soldiers came with drawn sabres into the apartment of Madame de Boursonne (former lady-in-waiting to Mesdames), who was very ill from hemorrhage, and had a constant fever. They went up to her bed, examined her closely, and said aloud 'that they would not have the trouble of visiting her long.' She came near dying after they went out. These kind fellow-citizens frequently had the goodness to forget to come to see me, because they knew that my cell was somewhat apart from the others.

Suddenly a party of forty prisoners were set at liberty in accordance with a command from their communes, under a law which granted the communes this right. There was general rejoicing among those who departed, and sweet hope for those who remained; but it was seen that by this means the prisons would be emptied, and the law was repealed. I was glad to take leave of two good Sisters of Charity from Noyon, thinking of all they would do for the poor whom they cared for so tenderly; but scarcely had a few prisoners been set at liberty when a larger number came to replace them. The districts of Beauvais, Noyon, Senlis, and Compiègne were most zealous in gathering recruits. We never had any vacancies. One day I met an old nun whom I did not know, bent with age and infirmities, who seemed to be suffering terrible pain in the side of her face. One of her companions told me that as she was getting into the wagon which brought her to Chantilly she made the sign of the cross; and one of the soldiers of the escort was so indignant that he gave her a frightful blow on her cheek which broke several of her teeth. How horrible! I took great pleasure in visiting these holy virgins, who were inconsolable at being compelled to leave their retreats where peace and innocence reigned. In order to console them for this, they were lodged so close to the coarsest men in the house that they constantly heard things said which made them very unhappy. They endured their strange and terrible situation with perfect resignation, and never failed to read their office as though they were in their convent.

My companions in misfortune differed very much; there were some who, in the hope of obtaining their liberty, undertook the rôle of informer. Several of them tried to sound me; they were not rewarded for their trouble. When they told me tales I would not listen, but immediately changed the conversation.

One thing which astonishes me as I look back is how little I suffered from *ennui* during my captivity. My thoughts were confined within a very narrow sphere. They dwelt upon my regret at being separated from those I loved and upon the needs of my daily life. The want of exercise, which is absolutely necessary to me from habits contracted in my childhood, gave me too great fulness of blood. I had violent rushes of blood to the head, and also rheumatism. Once on awakening I felt so stunned that I called the hospital nurse, who lodged near me. She thought I was dying, and went for help. This condition, which was really dangerous, was relieved by vomiting. I fell asleep; and when I woke I found myself surrounded by kind people, to whom I acknowledged my gratitude, and then burst into tears. They did not know what to make of it. I excused myself, and explained to them that once several years before I had had a similar attack, when I was surrounded by friends and relatives, and now I was terribly alone. I regained my composure, and then went out into the air.

The weak condition to which I was reduced made me unable to restrain the feelings and emotions which these sad memories aroused, though generally I have an aversion to speaking of what grieves me. The health officer of the prison was sent for; he was a violent revolutionist, small, very dark, uneducated, and dressed in a *carmagnole*, the uniform of the *sans-culottes*. Being difficult to bleed, I dared not have him bleed me, although I was in great need of it. He put leeches on my neck, which eased the pains in my head.

Very disturbing news reached us from Paris, and those were the only tidings which could come to us. It was reported that we were to be interrogated by means of blanks, which must be filled up. I had a great dread of this kind of torture on account of my love of truth, which might compromise both myself and others. Heaven did not allow them to realize this base project.

One of the prisoners died from the mistaken treatment of that imbecile surgeon, who, without asking him if he had hernia, gave him an emetic, which caused his death in twenty-four hours.

The treatment of the sick was terrible; no medicine was given them, no one was appointed to nurse them, and even the prisoners were forbidden to show them any attention. I once saw five cases of putrid fever in one room. A respectable girl from Crépy, who stayed in the apartment, was obliged to spend every night waiting on the patients. A good schoolmaster, who also was in the room, helped her as well as he could. I have seen him since, with great pleasure, and I entertain a real esteem for him.

Madame de Boursonne, who had recovered from her illness, and from the visit of the revolutionists, heard that Monsieur d'Ecquevilly, her father, was dying at Amiens. One may imagine her great desire to go to him and hear his last words; but an insurmountable barrier was placed between us and those dear to us. She could only hope to hear frequently from him, being very near him; but our keeper, Perdrix, refused even this, and kept all letters addressed to her. After a fortnight of terrible suspense had passed, he sent for her to come to him; this was for the purpose of reading to her, in the presence of every one, the letter announcing the death of her father, without even allowing her to have it, which at least would have given her the consolation of learning the details. Poor Madame de Boursonne was in a terrible state. I did everything in my power for her, and took her back to her own room.

One day as I was sitting alone in my chamber some officers of our guard came in with Monsieur Lambert, the Commissioner of War. The dread of something frightful was the first thing that flashed across my mind; but I was mistaken in my fear. This Monsieur Lambert, to whom I had rendered services under the old régime, had expressed a desire to see the place and my little cell. I made no sign of recognition because of the fear I had always had since the Revolution of compromising those who wished me well. When the officers were going out he let them pass before him, and said to me that if I had need of his services and wished to send off any letters he would take charge of them, and would be delighted to do me any kindness. I cannot tell how touched I was by this proposition, which, however, I was unwilling to accept. During the Reign of Terror the slightest kindness offered to persons of our rank was so dangerous that I still feel grateful to him for his good will.

Perdrix did not spoil us. Several of us asked him for a copy of our entry in the jail-book; this seemed a small favour, but we could not obtain it. The clerk of the commune of Chantilly came quite frequently to the château, in order to give certificates of residence. He showed a sort of interest in the prisoners. Whenever they were not harshly treated it was on account of the natural amiability of individuals. Monsieur Wallon, of Beauvais, having confidence in the clerk, commissioned him to procure some money for him; he accepted the commission graciously, and disappeared. I never should have imagined it necessary to have one's residence in a prison certified. It seemed to me that to make a list of those who were there would have been sufficient; but it turned out very well for me that I took the precaution I thought superfluous, as I was inscribed upon the list of *émigrés* during my imprisonment.

I was not pleased at the reception given a fat curate from Noyon who had apostatized, and had denounced and caused to be imprisoned a good many of our fellow-prisoners. He was hooted at from the head of any stairway he attempted to ascend; and the crowd pushed him back, and used syringes upon him. I was very sorry to see a man so lost to principle among us; but I should have preferred not to see any unfortunate being insulted. Any one is unfortunate who has lost his liberty; and those who are wicked are the most to be pitied under such circumstances. I was sorry also for those who, instead of thinking of more serious things, fed themselves with vain hopes concerning the future, and the possibility of shaking off their fetters.

I grew accustomed to living at Chantilly, and my companions in misfortune treated me with great kindness. Madame de Séguier and Mademoiselle le Caron de Troupure, now Madame Flomond, both amiable and excellent women, were a great comfort to me. I tried to help those who needed courage. The Coincy family, who lodged near me, were good company. I had great consolation from a religious point of view. A venerable priest undertook to confess me, and even to give me the communion. He had had the courage to bring a large supply of consecrated wafers, and had kept them in spite of the danger he ran should the fact have been discovered.

I was quite content with my fate, since I was compelled to endure a hard one. I could not have asked to be in a better prison; Providence had placed me there, and six months sojourn had accustomed me to it.

Toward the end of March, 1794, I received a letter from my mother, full of kindness, but which grieved me very much. She told me that she had thought it astonishing that I made no application to the government commissioners who came to Chantilly, to be allowed to join her. This intimation seemed to be an order and a command of Providence which altered my destiny. I immediately inquired when Citizen Martin, who inspected our house, was to come. I presented him a petition, asking to be sent to the Luxembourg by the first train destined for Paris. He assented, and then occupied himself in getting ready a most atrocious party, composed of young girls who were torn from the arms of their mothers without knowing for what they were destined.

Many persons believed, and it was really talked of, that the intentions of the Terrorists was to marry them to *sans-culottes*. To this party were added some priests, women, laymen, etc. The unhappy mothers were in despair. I was a witness of the scene with Madame de Pons (formerly Vicomtesse) at Perdrix's apartments. She fell on her knees before him and before Martin; she said everything to them that the desperation of such a moment could suggest, using the most touching expressions; they would listen to nothing. She fell fainting at their feet. After she recovered her consciousness, she implored to be permitted at least to follow her daughter; they refused her.

I forgot to say that a moment before Madame de Pons came to see Perdrix the latter had sent for her daughter, and in the presence of Martin and two gendarmes said to her,

'What is your name?'

'Pons.'

'Yes, but give your Christian names.'

'You should speak to my mother; I will go for her.'

'No, no; I ask you for your names.'

'There they are. May I know what use you have for them?'

'You will leave here with other prisoners to-morrow, to go to another prison.'

'Without mamma! O God! What will be my fate?'

'Go, or I will have you carried out.'

Madame de Pons wrote several letters to Martin, asking only for a delay; she offered all her property to the Republic; and the only answer she received was, 'Your daughter must go!'

I busied myself in arranging my trunks and packing them for the Luxembourg, so as to have with me only what was strictly necessary. On the 3d of April, 1794, we were told to hold ourselves in readiness to leave the next day or the day following, as the carriages were expected. My travelling companions were in despair at leaving their parents, but I delighted at going to see mine once more; every one said pleasant things to me. I received many testimonials of interest and regret from the prisoners. There were some from whom I was grieved to part, and a secret presentiment (though generally I do not believe in them) seemed to warn me that the reunion with my parents would never be effected. The days of the 3d and 4th were passed in leave-taking. I did not know that the train was to start early on the 5th, the anniversary of the birth of my son. I was summoned at ten o'clock in the morning. I found the wagons almost full; consequently I had a wretched seat next a vile woman who boasted of being a friend of Robespierre, and told us that she would receive on the way some marks of public interest. She sat almost half on top of me; and to add to our suffering, the straw which is usually put in the bottom of the carts for calves, was left out. When we left, the courtyard was filled with our companions in misery, who were mourning and sighing over our fate. They concealed their tears, fearing to let them be seen.

Our procession stopped as it passed out of the gate, in order to have the roll-call, lest some prisoner should have escaped; we were as accustomed to it as the soldiers were. We were surrounded by the National Guard, and remained an hour under the windows of the château, in sight of mothers disconsolate at the removal of their daughters, and who, with their hands raised to heaven, were giving them their blessings. That sad sight is still distinctly before me. How many of those who gave those blessings and of those who looked on were sacrificed on the scaffold! I should like to be able to depict and describe fully all that terrible and touching scene, but I cannot. As for me I was terribly overcome, but I struggled to hide it.

The train was put in command of a printer's apprentice from Beauvais, who went ahead of us. The first cart was filled with young girls, the second with women, and three others with men. The vehicles were surrounded by musketeers. We started at eleven o'clock in the morning, in very bad weather. A terribly cold wind was blowing, and there were no covers to our wagons.

At the entrances of towns and villages our escort was gathered together, and we entered with dignity, drums beating.

In some places, particularly at Creil-sur-Oise, gestures indicating the cutting off of the head were made to us. In a village called La Mortaye a dozen persons suddenly appeared, who came to see my heavy neighbour, and whispered to her that she would not be much longer in prison.

When we reached Mesnil-Aubry we were made to get out at an inn,—that is, the women and young girls at one, and the men at another. It was Saturday. I obtained the favour of an omelette. Immediately after dinner it was demanded of us that we should pay on the spot the expenses of our removal; I refused to do this, saying truly that I had no money. Mademoiselle de Pons obeyed, and gave a hundred and ninety-two francs. The women whose husbands were in the train asked permission to go to see them while the horses were resting, but could not obtain it. The notorious Martin, of whom I have already had occasion to speak several times, came to inspect us, and placed himself at the head of our train when it started off. He was in a gilded *berline*, drawn by post horses, and seated in front was a small clerk, about twelve years old. I said to myself, 'Unfortunate child, what an education this Terrorism is!' Along the way he reviewed us as though he were a superior officer, going from end to end of our melancholy column, to see if it was coming up in order. Sometimes our horses began to trot, and we were terribly jolted. As we were approaching Paris, my side, which was pressed against the wagon, with nothing between, began to hurt me very much. My love of books, and the fear of being without them, had caused me to fill two pairs of pockets with them, and they thumped against me. If we had been obliged to go any farther I should have been compelled to change my position, but I could not make up my mind to ask any favour of the friend of Robespierre.

The train stopped about eight o'clock in the evening at St. Denis. Martin left us. The officer of the guard separated the men from the women, in order to take the former to the Luxembourg. It began to rain, and continued until we reached Paris. Our conductors did not know the streets. We implored them to tell us where we were going; their reply was that they knew nothing about it. After driving us around until eleven o'clock in the darkness, they came to the gates of the Madelonnettes. We had great difficulty in making the porter hear, and he said that no women were received in that house, that Ste. Pélagie, which was set apart for them, was quite full, but that we would find room in the Plessis, an old college of the University, Rue St. Jacques, next to that of Louis-le-Grand. Our guards, who were but human, were overcome with fatigue, and impatient to put us down in some prison or other. I saw that we were taking the way to the Conciergerie; then frightful thoughts rushed over me, and also a suspicion that our end was near at hand if we were to be confined there. But we passed by without stopping, and I felt more tranquil the remainder of the way.

The gate of the Collège du Plessis was the end of our journey. Our conductor knocked there a long time without attracting any notice; perhaps no one heard, or perhaps the porter did not wish to be aroused. It was one o'clock. At last in the darkness the gates were opened; we did not know where we were. I feared lest the cart in which the young girls were had been separated from the train. I perceived it as we were entering the courtyard, and had a sad satisfaction in seeing them again even in so wretched a place.

We passed under an archway and stopped. Our guards were kind enough to assist us to descend from our rude vehicles; we should scarcely have had strength to do so without their help, weary and bruised as we were from our fourteen hours' journey.

The first object to attract my attention was a man dressed in a sort of dressing-gown, who said he was the porter. He had an enormous bunch of keys hanging from his belt, and carried a lantern, by the light of which I saw gratings, enormous bars of iron, heaps of stone and other materials,—in short, the general appearance of a prison which was being enlarged. We were taken through several gratings, and were immediately surrounded by drunken jailers,—great heavily built men, half naked, with their sleeves rolled up, and red caps on their heads, and whose speech was suited to their costumes. I trembled at the sight of these creatures, who seemed to wish to be familiar with our young girls. I immediately proposed to the ladies who came with me that we should each take one of them under our care, so as to protect them against this vulgar herd. They agreed to my proposition. Mademoiselle de Pons, who has since married Monsieur de Tourzel, fell to my charge. I warned her not to get behind me, but to hold on to my dress, and not leave me for a moment. One of the jailers, who was a regular Goliath, began to read the list of those who composed our train, and could scarcely decipher it. Detention in the gate-house being impossible, he conducted us to a large hall where there was not a single pane of glass in the windows, and only wooden benches to sit on. We were suffering terribly from thirst; the worst of the jailers, named Baptiste, brought us a bucket of water, which we hailed with intense delight. A moment after he brought another for other purposes. The visit of this man, Baptiste, was accompanied by speeches such as we had never before heard, and which filled me with horror, particularly on account of our young friends. About two o'clock in the morning our keeper appeared; he had been absent when we arrived. His name was Haly; his face was pale and livid. He smiled as he saw the young girls, and said to them, 'My children, you have not yet been entered in the jail-book. I keep you here only for humanity's sake. This house is at the disposal of the public accuser, Fouquier-Tinville, and is only destined for the anti-revolutionists; you do not seem to be such. To-morrow your report will be made out, and I will inform you of your destination.'

Every one tried to speak to him. I had my turn, and told him that as I had never been denounced I was only to be classed among the suspected; that I ought not to be kept in his prison; and that I had left Chantilly in order to be transferred to the Luxembourg. I implored him to have me sent there. Several persons told him he had no right to keep us; he paid no attention to what they said, and had the mattresses, which had been brought in the wagons, brought in. I had not taken the precaution to bring one, and consequently passed the night seated on a small wooden bench, occupied in trying to conceal the small amount of paper money I had with me. I did not sleep a moment; neither did my companions. As the day dawned I saw with delight that our young girls were sleeping sweetly and peacefully. I said to myself, 'At their age one has had neither the experience of misfortune nor the anxiety born of foresight.' The thought of seeing my parents during the day cheered my sad heart. It was extremely cold. Baptiste came in, accompanied by several of his comrades, who regarded us with a ferocious sort of pleasure, judging that we were good recruits for their house, and that they would have a good share of our purses. One of them, a former lackey of Madame de Narbonne, recognized me, and behaved very properly toward me. A gendarme, whose name I never learned, came up to me and whispered in my ear, 'Hide your money and your jewels. They will leave you only fifty francs in paper money, and will take away your knives and your scissors.' I thanked him, and he retired. Although the great mental agony we endured caused us to pay but little heed to our physical needs, we nevertheless became extremely hungry. We had taken nothing to eat since the day before, and had endured excessive physical and mental fatigue. We petitioned our jailers for food, and after keeping us waiting two hours they brought us some coffee and chocolate. I breakfasted with the pleasant feeling of alleviating suffering for a moment at least. Martin came in afterward to get a cloak which had been lent to Madame de Vassy; he looked at us sternly. Several went up to him to ask something of him, among them the young girls, who were extremely anxious to let their mothers know what had become of them. They gave him some notes for this purpose, but these never reached their destination.

I implored the said Martin (I may speak of him in this way under the circumstances) to send me to the Luxembourg; he gave me some hope, but I regarded it as slender. His visit was soon over. Up to this time the National Guard of Chantilly had remained with us; it was now replaced by jailers who never left us. A new face appeared; it was an inspector named Grandpré, who had quite a pleasing countenance. Being astonished at seeing us in this prison, and a little touched by our forlorn situation, he promised to endeavour to have us transferred to a house for suspected persons, and me in particular to the Luxembourg. Haly, our keeper, now came in, and said that our fate had been decided,—that we were entered on the jail-book as agitators and as refractory to discipline at the house at Chantilly. A cry of surprise and grief arose, but our keeper was deaf to all complaints. My companions deserved such terms as little as I did; and I declare that after my conduct there, submitting as I did to all the wishes of the commissioners, meddling with nothing, complaining of nothing, being taken to Paris at my own request, I was more completely astonished than I can express. The false accusations were certainly the least of my woes,—innocence easily consoles itself; but to see myself deprived of the delight of rejoining my parents made my heart ache, and all the more because I was very sure that they would fully share my sorrow.

We were obliged to resign ourselves to remaining under the immediate rule of Fouquier-Tinville, shut up with those directly accused, and consequently treated more severely than the suspected. We remained fifteen hours in that hall, into which we had been thrown rather than conducted. If we went out for necessary purposes we were escorted by two musketeers; most of us preferred to suffer rather than take such a promenade. The day wore away; we saw a movement among our jailers. Following the example of one of my pious companions, I had got into a corner of the hall to recite my mass and office. It was Passion Sunday; following the example of our divine Master we forgave insult, and tried to imitate his patience.

We were given to understand that we could write and receive letters, a pleasure of which we had been deprived at Chantilly. Mademoiselle de Pons received one letter, which gave us some little hope. Toward evening a rumour spread that we were to be searched and put in lodgings. We sought new means of concealing our watches and our paper money. The keeper ordered us to appear before him two by two to be registered; he then informed us that it was the custom of the house to turn over to him all scissors, knives, forks, and watches, because such things could be used to file away the bars. Afterward he demanded all our jewels and money with the exception of fifty francs in *assignats*. He had the politeness not to search us, saying that he would dispense with that out of respect for us. I gave up to him all he required, except a few *assignats* and a small and very ugly brass clock, which was precious to me because it had sounded in my hearing the last hours of the lives of my dear friends Mesdames de Chaulnes and de Mailly. The keeper would not leave it with me, in spite of the sorrow I assured him I felt in giving it up, alleging the same reason that he gave when he demanded the watches. When this agreeable operation was over we were told to follow the jailers. They made us mount to the very top of the building, passing through a grating on each floor, fastened by enormous bolts and guarded by four men. We had to go through these two at a time.

At last we reached our own rooms. Mademoiselle de Pons had not left my side since we reached Plessis; we took the measure of our habitation, and found that with some management we had room enough for two beds, placing the head of one at the foot of the other. This sweet girl burst into tears when she saw our poor little establishment, sat down on a mattress beside me, and said, 'We shall surely die. It is impossible to live in such a contracted place. O God! may none of my friends ever come here!'

I did my best to arouse her courage, which had quite vanished, and to remove her dislike at living so intimately with an old woman by assuring her that I had no disease. Our furniture consisted of two chairs; our mattresses were on the floor, and the wall served as our pillow. Fortunately it was freshly whitened, and consequently clean. The bolts were fastened,— a sad moment; for the sound they made told us that until morning, no matter what happened, it was impossible for us to receive any assistance. We were told that a jailer of the guard would answer if we called; but I heard one of my neighbours cry all night with pain, and no one went to help her.

My first night's rest was excellent. The intense fatigue I had suffered the preceding days made me sleep. My young companion slept soundly and late. When daylight appeared I found we had a fine view; I could see the whole city of Paris. I reflected sadly upon the terrible condition of my unhappy country, once so far-famed as a place where one could spend peaceful, happy days. I thought of all the horrors which were being committed there; the tears rose to my eyes, but I dried them quickly so as not to discourage Mademoiselle de Pons when she first awakened.

About eight o'clock in the morning the bolts were drawn and the keeper, Haly, came in, followed by an enormous dog. This strange man greeted us as though we were in one of the old-time châteaux where abundance, peace, and pleasure reigned. He even seemed astonished that we were not charmed with the pleasant lodgings he had given us. After he was gone, and our companions' bolts were drawn, we eagerly gathered together, and had no trouble in finding one another, as the corridor on which we were lodged was only three feet wide. The first thing to be done was to arrange about our meals. It was only after repeated requests that we received permission to go down six steps to get water. The jailer who had charge of us, as well as his comrades, assumed the title of warden, thinking thus to render their office more honourable. There were three classes of them, and almost all were drunkards, selfish, rapacious, lying, while a few were absolutely ferocious. We specially noticed one of them, who had taken part in the massacre of the 2d of September, 1792. This man, who at this time was our despot, was a sculptor; and I was astonished that he should have accepted so miserable an employment. After he had granted us permission to go for water, the need of having something to eat made itself felt. The mess-table had not then been established. I inquired how we could procure provisions at a moderate price. An eating-house keeper sent us our dinner; but before he could reach the floor on which we lodged, which was the highest in the house, the food he carried was often taken from him as he passed along on the other floors. Finding that I could not possibly live in this way, I sent to learn whether my dinner could be sent me every day from my own house.

Lucas, my father's former clerk, was very anxious that this should be done; but it was very difficult to find any one in the house who was willing to bring it to me, as it was considered a dangerous thing to do, and not very 'civic'. At last an old postilion named Lerot, whose name I mention with gratitude, had the courage to undertake it. A neighbour of the Hôtel Mouchy, said openly in the street, when she saw him go by, that it was not worth while taking me anything to eat because I was going to be guillotined. Two respectable ladies clubbed together with me, and we divided our provisions,—they furnishing some also; and we set about getting them cooked. Mademoiselle de Pons did not find our fare good enough, and joined with a woman from Beauvais, and two young girls.

I enter into minute details which would be very tiresome if this memoir was intended to be read by strangers; but it is for my own relatives that it is written, and I am too sure of the interest they take in what I have suffered to omit to mention the least thing.

The rules of our prison were extremely strict. At eight o'clock in the morning the keepers opened the doors; this was a truly agreeable moment,—if I may use such an expression in such a connection; then they wrote our names on the registers, but being so little accustomed to such matters they never made the list as it should be, and so were obliged to have the roll-call two or three times a day. One moment they ordered us to remain inside our rooms, and another we were told to stand like sentinels at our doors. The locking up, and ascertaining that each prisoner was in her place, seemed a more solemn affair. The keeper, followed by the turnkeys, gendarmes, and some large dogs, came about ten o'clock in the evening or at midnight. This goodly company made pleasing jokes and a great deal of noise. I always pretended to be asleep, and made no reply to what they said. It seemed sad that our sleep, which alone had the power to cause us to forget our troubles, should be interrupted by that sound which most quickly recalled them.

During the first days after our arrival we spent our time mostly in sending petitions to Fouquier-Tinville, asking to be reunited to our families. We have since learned that not one of them reached him. I eagerly sought for some opportunity of sending or receiving communications from my parents. At last I discovered that in sending some trifling thing to the Luxembourg I could add two or three lines, which at least served to say we were alive. The notes were sent open, and passed through the hands of the registrars and jailers of Plessis and the Luxembourg. I suffered intensely at having to inform my parents that I should not have the consolation of joining them; they tenderly expressed their deep regret for this. The sight of their handwriting, after having been so long deprived of it, moved me profoundly; I received a few words from them every two or three days.

The commissioner, Grandpré, fearing lest our crowded condition should cause sickness, proposed that we should take the air in the courtyard. We had a great aversion to going down a hundred steps, passing six grated iron doors, preceded, accompanied, and followed by keepers. We refused to do it for some time. Then he told us that if we paid no regard to his request we should be charged with aristocratic opinions; consequently, we were obliged to yield, and take the walk. The place appointed for our promenade was very confined, enclosed by plank fences, and surrounded by gendarmes, who kept their eyes upon us. We found there about twenty women who had come from the Conciergerie, and who were lodged under us without our knowing anything about it. After conversing with them our fears were redoubled; for they gave us a most fearful account of that terrible prison, which has been called the anti-chamber of death. They told us that every day a large number of victims for the scaffold were sent from there, and that our house was considered a sort of annex to the Conciergerie. We were entirely ignorant of what was going on outside our cells. Madame de Vassy, a pupil of J. J. Rousseau, and daughter of Monsieur de Girardin, had induced a jailer named Launay, the best of our keepers, to bring her some newspapers; but this was found out, and was considered an unpardonable crime. He was taken to another prison and put in irons, and but for the death of Robespierre would have perished. This man, who is still living, actually wept when he took us out on our compulsory airing, which rather seemed like leading out a pack of dogs. Rain or shine we were taken out for the prescribed time. If some of us wished to go in sooner than others, we were forbidden to do so, and we were taken out whenever our keepers chose. The men who lodged near the stairway were obliged to retire when we passed in front of their gratings; but their windows looked out upon the space where we were allowed, or rather ordered, to walk, and there they often recognized their wives and children,—all those whom they loved, and of whose very existence they were ignorant.

Only prisoners from Chantilly were now lodged on our corridor. Among those who came from the Conciergerie were Mesdames de Grimaldi and de Bussy, from whom we had a full account of all the horrors which were being enacted there. A few days later Madame de Bussy was carried off, to be indicted by the Revolutionary tribunal; but her case was not pressed, and she returned to Plessis. We were just congratulating her on the subject when she was sent for again, and led to the scaffold. She had scarcely gone when the jailers seized upon all her effects, and tried to sell them to us,—an incident which shocked us greatly. We repelled their disgusting proposition with horror.

The condition of affairs grew worse every day. Parties came to us from all the Departments; our prison was terribly crowded; the faces constantly changed. Those who arrived told us of the death of persons of the highest reputation. We questioned the keeper, but he would give no explanation of the vague rumours which reached us. I implored him once more to effect my reunion with my parents, but with no result. He replied to my earnest solicitations compassionately, 'You do not know what you are asking; you would certainly not be better off at the Luxembourg.' He seemed to foresee the horrors which were to take place there. Alas! I was not thinking of the strictness of the prison rule, but of the longings of my own heart.

A garden was given us for our promenade-ground instead of the courtyard surrounded by the plank fence. One day as I was passing very near the building in which we were living, accompanied by Mesdemoiselles de Pons and Titon, I saw them pick up a scrap of paper which was thrown out of the vent-hole of an underground apartment, the window of which they had neglected to close. There were a few lines written upon it, which were almost illegible, but which we made out to be, 'Three unfortunate beings, completely destitute, implore your pity.' The paper was tied to a string, which was withdrawn. Mademoiselle de Pons, much moved, said to her companion, 'Is it possible that we are surrounded by such miserable beings?' She asked my permission to throw them some money, and I granted it. She wrapped it in a tiny package, and pretended to pick up a stone, while Mademoiselle Titon let it drop quietly into the dungeon. We heard a clapping of hands. The eyes of the young girls filled with tears; and the evening was passed in the satisfied feeling that they had been able, for a moment at least, to render the situation of those suffering creatures less wretched.

We never learned what became of them.

A month had passed since we left Chantilly when a party arrived, among whom was Madame de Pons, to whom I restored the precious charge which I had been so happy as to keep for her; I was then left in sole possession of my room, which I enjoyed very much. I was informed that it was proposed to separate the suspected persons from those indicted by the Revolutionary tribunal, and to place us in a building facing that we were now occupying. This change seemed so advantageous to us that we urged the keeper to carry it out as quickly as possible. To do him justice, he behaved very well on this occasion, using his influence with the terrible Fouquier-Tinville to prevent our being mistaken for the indicted prisoners, and to effect our removal without delay. I regretted for a moment the loss of the beautiful view from my apartment; all the fine buildings in Paris were before me,—the cathedral, St. Sulpice, the Val-de-Grâce, etc. I remembered that on Easter Day, as I was grieving over the thought that the holy sacrifice was no longer offered up in those temples made so venerable by their antiquity, and the prayers of the faithful, I joined in the prayers of those whose faith was strong, and who were sharing my sad thoughts, and found that I was really more edified than I had often been on that holy day when at the foot of the altar.

At last the order came for us to leave our apartments, and carry our effects with us. One person was sufficient to assist me in my moving; a wretched pallet, a straw chair, and a few dishes composed my only furniture. The moment of our departure was very trying to those who remained still under the power of the public accuser. Several of them wept when we left them. The separation was final.

When I reached my new prison it seemed to me a mansion, since there were only two gratings instead of six, as before; and as the men were entirely separated from the women, we were allowed to go all over the building, from top to bottom, without a keeper. I was lodged on the fifth floor, in what was called formerly 'the philosophers' warming-place'. The names of the scholars were, as is customary, written in charcoal on the walls; I recognized a few of them. There was a fireplace in this pretty room, and I think it was the only one in the corridor. It was immediately made use of to warm all my neighbours' coffee-pots, which occasioned a continual procession not at all agreeable.

Before my detention, I had thought that a prison would be at least a place of repose, where I could give myself up to study; but this was not the case at all, at least not in those where I stayed. Every moment the keeper, the jailers, the turnkeys, the purveyors, etc., came in. We were made to go down to the clerk's office to attend to our commissions. I could not read one single hour without interruption. One thing which I have heard spoken of, and which I have certainly verified, is the habit prisoners have of being destructive. It arises from their standing in need of a thousand things. I had no shovel, so I broke a piece of slating and used it for one; I took a floor-tile for a lid. It was very difficult to procure wood, so I burned up my chairs. We could not send a keeper down-stairs without paying him a hundred sous.

In spite of the admiration inspired by my new dwelling-place, I was forced to sigh for the one I had left. We slept where the plaster was quite fresh, which gave me such a raw sensation in my throat that I could swallow nothing but milk. On the stairways there was a very unwholesome smell of oil; all the windows, above and below, had been grated, and boards adjusted, so as to make it impossible to throw letters out. The outer aspect of our building was frightful. We lost by our transfer the promenade in the garden, and had instead one no better than in the courtyard at Plessis, so that one could not make up one's mind to go out except when it was absolutely necessary to go in the open air. The men and women went there at different hours. They were shut in on every side; and walls had been erected so that the prisoners could not be seen by their neighbours, and could make no sign to them. One little alley-way, however, which it was impossible to shut out from our view, allowed us to see human beings at liberty, or who at least believed themselves to be. The windows which procured this little view for us were very much sought after and always occupied. Persons interested in the prisoners came to assure themselves of our existence. Our numbers increased each day, and brought us some detestable recruits. I had very near me some vulgar creatures,—young women from the Rue de Chartres, some persons with the itch, the hangman's mistress, and a drunken creature, who said she was a person of quality belonging to the family of Désarmoise, to whom in manner at any rate she bore not the slightest resemblance. She assumed the right to come into our rooms every day, make a great noise, and deliver herself of the most abusive language, for which she afterward asked pardon. I was, of course, very much touched by her repentance, but her visits were still very disagreeable to me. Another of my neighbours, a lady of the court, was insane; and unfortunately for me, she took a great fancy to me. She lay down to sleep one day just in my doorway, and could only be gotten away by force. The sort of care that I was obliged to take of her was as disagreeable as it was fatiguing, and it was a real calamity. One of her fancies was to write to Robespierre. I suppose her letters suffered the same fate as ours,—never to reach their destination. Only the two lines added to the requests which we made for necessary things ever found favour at the clerk's office.

The mess-table, the nature of which we had experienced at Chantilly, was established. We were placed in the rhetoric class-room, and grouped at tables of twelve covers each. Each of us had a wooden spoon, but no fork; and we were given to understand that the latter was a dangerous thing. We also had a wooden bowl given us from which to eat our soup; and I have kept it as a curiosity. I never used it. It seemed as though pains had been taken to do everything which could excite our disgust. The tables had no cloths, and were never washed; as a great deal of wine was spilled the smell was insupportable. Hairs were often found in the food; and the dirtiest of the prisoners were detailed to wait upon us. Pigs ran about the refectory while we were at dinner. A notice was posted one day, saying that it was only necessary to give us enough to keep us alive.

Supper was entirely done away with. Mesdames de Courteilles, de Rochechouart, and de Richelieu ate with the lowest creatures, and Madame and Mademoiselle de Pons with Mademoiselle Dervieux, of the Opera, a negress, and what were called feminine *sans-culottes*.

The men ate in another refectory. My mess-mates were hard to please in the matter of food, among them the daughter of one of the Duke of Bourbon's grooms. Such people were never content. The keeper, angry one day because they tried to throw their plates in his face, pointed me out to the commissioner who examined us, as well as others of my class, and said, 'You can ask those ladies; they never complain of anything.' He greatly preferred to have charge of us than of the common people. The keepers at Plessis were not at all like those at Chantilly, who were kind, attentive, obliging and attached to us. Those at Plessis persecuted us to get money, demanded services of us, and reproached us when we had two garments for not giving them one of them. They were very hard to get along with. I often served them as secretary in writing to their relatives or making applications. Once while doing something of this sort a very amusing thing happened to Madame de la Fayette. A woman asked her to compose a petition for her, which she did immediately, with the readiness and kindness which characterized her. But as her handwriting was bad, she charged the person to have it copied; and she had the stupidity to send it to a prisoner, who, good patriot that he was, was indignant at the want of civism evinced in it, and sent it back with some words effaced, and the following remarks: 'This petition is aristocratic; one never uses such phraseology. This is not civic; it has the odour of a château. This person does not know how to draw up a petition,' etc.

We laughed a great deal at the severe criticism aroused by this kind action.

A convoy from La Force brought Madame de la Fayette to us at Plessis. The van-guard was composed of Madame des Réaux, who was eighty-four years old, Madame de Machaut, and other women who were at least seventy. These were, as a great favour, put into a carriage; the others, as was the custom, came in a cart. It was a long time before they were put into lodgings, and we were allowed to approach them. At last I was able to see one of my cousins, who found the rules in this prison less severe than in the one from which she came; and all the girls of the street from Paris collected there presented a spectacle so indecent that one so pure as she could scarcely endure it. Besides, she slept in a room where there were four other persons whom she did not know; I was able to get another room for her, which she thought quite palatial. She has often told me of the extreme pleasure she felt on awaking and finding herself alone. The room was so small that she could not put a chair between her bed and the wall; there was fortunately a recess, however, where with some trouble she could sit down. Having Madame de la Fayette so near me was very pleasant. Her virtues and kindliness, which had suffered no change from the life she had been compelled to live during the first years of the Revolution, the possibility of opening my heart to her with regard to my family, concerning my anxiety for whom I had never spoken to any one, did me much good; we wept together over her own fate. She seemed to me to be much less prepared than I was for the general and particular evils which threatened us. She thought, for instance, that she could defend her cause and that of her husband before the Revolutionary tribunal, and that only those were in danger who had committed some serious or trifling injury to the Republic. It took me at least a fortnight to set her right on this subject, and enable her to realize her true situation; but, indeed, what passed before our eyes was more eloquent than anything I could say.

The number of victims carried off became larger and larger; they generally went away during the time we were taking our walk in the courtyard. It seems to me now, that I can see the unfortunate Monsieur Titon, a counsellor in the parliament of Paris, as he passed beneath the windows of the room of his wife and daughter, who were not even permitted to bid him a last farewell. He went out at five o'clock in the evening, and the next day at noon he was dead. Carts and Fouquier-Tinville's carriage arrived at all hours, and were crowded with the accused. This man's coachman was well worthy of such a master; while the victims were getting into the wagon he drummed out dancing tunes, and his costume was that of a Merry Andrew. It is almost impossible to describe the terror excited by the opening of the great gate, especially when it was repeated several times a day. I can hear now the sound of the drum beating. The bailiffs of the Revolutionary tribunal went before the wagons with their hands full of warrants. Then there was a moment of deathlike silence. Every one thought the fatal order had come for him; faces were filled with terror, hearts and minds overwhelmed with fright. The bailiffs went up into the corridors to call for those who were to go off, and only allowed them a quarter of an hour to prepare. Each bade the other an eternal farewell; we were in a stunned condition, being only sure of living from ten o'clock in the morning until seven o'clock in the evening. Sleep was light when one suffered such anxiety, and was frequently interrupted by the arrival of convoys. That containing the famous prisoners from Nantais created a great sensation. It was the custom to receive the prisoners with lighted torches; and the keeper, accompanied by jailers and big dogs, dragged the poor prisoners from the wagons in the roughest manner. They were so much afraid of losing some of the prisoners that they called the roll two or three times in succession, then put them in the "mouse-trap,"—a new name for a receiving-place. There was no calculation as to whether there was room enough in the house; room was made: and there have been as many, so we have been assured, as seventeen hundred at one time in the colleges of Plessis and Louis-le-Grand. Twenty-five persons were put in the same room, even in the *entresols*, with grated windows. The severity of the treatment increased constantly. One day about three o'clock in the afternoon I heard my bolts shot to, and could not understand the reason; it was unusual. It was on account of a servant having thrown water out of a window into the courtyard, after having been forbidden; and for this great crime we were punished.

We were not allowed to have any light in our rooms; this was a very great privation. To room in front of a street lamp was a great piece of good fortune. In the corridors were placed chaffing-dishes, on which we warmed our suppers. Those of us who had fireplaces kept the fires bright, so as to give light. Some one would light a candle for a moment, then extinguish it the next, for fear of being punished. To eat with our fingers was intolerable. To go to the jailer every day to ask him to cut up our chocolate was neither amusing nor satisfactory. I remember a large penknife which belonged to Madame Vassy which was our delight. She was a lovely woman, bright and intelligent, and extremely obliging. She said she liked variety. She married, on leaving the prison, a Prussian, who took her to Berlin.

On the 18th of June I witnessed a heart-rending scene. I was in Madame de Pon's apartment, playing a game of chess with her, when some one came and called me; I went out. A person who felt an interest in Madame de Pon's daughter told me that her father had been transferred from the private hospital where he had been, to the Plessis, and that as he was getting out of the wagon he had received his bill of indictment; that he implored most earnestly to be allowed to see his daughter, but was refused, in order to avoid such a harrowing interview. The windows of the keeper's apartment opened directly upon the courtyard where Mademoiselle de Pons was then walking; they were ordered to be closed. Monsieur de Pons gave himself up to the most frenzied despair, saying that the most precious treasure he had in the world was taken from him. We did not know how to get his daughter out of the courtyard without arousing her suspicions. Haly had caused her to suspect that something was going on, by forbidding her to go under the windows on account of the arrival of some new prisoners. I made some pretext to persuade her to go into our building with one of my friends; and the latter led her to a place quite away from her unfortunate father. Then I returned to Madame de Pons's room, and from the change in my countenance she perceived that something had happened. I said nothing, but began playing chess again, in order to gain time to prepare her for it. The state of affairs between herself and her husband rendered this less terrible for her than for her daughter. She urged me to tell her the cause of my emotion. As Monsieur de Pons had been ill of consumption for a long time, I told her that he was about to die. She begged me not to tell her daughter of it, and I promised. This unhappy man was not sent for to be taken to the Conciergerie until nine o'clock in the evening, and consequently he was in the same building with his child for five hours without being able to take her in his arms, comfort her, or bid her a last farewell. He spent all of the time in seeking by threats and prayers to excite the compassion and interest of the keeper, telling him of her youth, of his affection for her, and that his last prayer was that happier days might be in store for her. He cast a farewell glance toward the courtyard, and then was led away. I spent the evening in extreme trouble and agitation; although I knew Monsieur de Pons only very slightly, the thought that he had not in his last agonized hours been able to see his daughter and bless her, and the grief I knew she would feel, all caused me to pass a terrible night. The young girl has since told me that she suspected that something sad was being concealed from her, by the embarrassment in our manner toward her. She came the next day as usual to my apartment to comb my thin white hair, and I could scarcely restrain my feelings while I was dressing when I remembered that her father was at that very moment before the tribunal or mounting the scaffold. She went away immediately. Madame de Pons had asked me to tell her the whole truth, and I had done so. She had sent for news of her husband's trial, and learned that he and also Messieurs de Laval, de Rohan-Soubise, de Monterrey, and fifty others had been condemned to death as conspirators against Robespierre, and were to be executed at the Grève, wearing red shirts, though these by law were required to be worn only by murderers. It seems that in order to make this so-called conspiracy more noted, the most celebrated names of the old régime, had been made use of, and that in fact those who bore them had never thought of conspiring.

All day means were employed to increase Mademoiselle de Pons's anxiety on account of her father's illness as she knew he was in great danger, and feared his end was approaching. She says in one of her prison memoirs, of which a few copies have been printed, that I asked permission of her mother to tell her of her father's death. She did not know that, on the contrary, it was Madame de Pons who earnestly implored me to undertake to break it to her, and that for a long time I refused. At last she gave me some very good reasons for doing so, and I consented. Mademoiselle de Pons, in whose presence I no longer concealed my emotion, suspected her misfortune. She questioned me; I made no reply, but threw my arms around her and burst into tears.

Another calamity befell us, the small-pox broke out. Madame des Réaux, eighty-four years old, died of it; and an only son also died, almost in sight of his father and mother, who were cruelly refused permission to go into another prison to weep over their unhappy child. They drank their cup to the dregs. Two very old ladies by the name of Machault were also attacked by this horrible disease, which naturally was greatly dreaded by all those who had not had it. Fortunately the contagion did not spread, which was extraordinary in a place where so many persons were crowded together. Besides, the manner in which the sick were treated was horrible. No money could procure medicine for them, or even a cup of tea. I saw a very strong woman die, who could have been cured with very little care. It required two days' negotiation to gain permission to have a warming-pan brought into the house. The prison surgeon was a Pole, named Markoski, who had come to Paris to study medicine, of which he was entirely ignorant. I needed to be bled; he found that it was difficult to do this in my arm. I let him try my foot, and he was successful. I pardoned his want of skill and his ignorance on account of his kindness of heart. He was really obliging; he brought us news of persons of our acquaintance who were imprisoned in other houses of arrest. And he was particularly kind to me because I gave him an account of the sick, and because, as I knew some medical phrases, I spared him the trouble of making out certificates of infirmity for persons who hoped by that means to escape close imprisonment; it was only necessary for him to sign what I had written. One day when I was feeling very badly, I said to myself, 'It would be so sweet to die in my bed.' What a terrible condition it is when one rejoices over an illness which may bring death!

I omitted to relate a very ridiculous incident. The day before the Feast of the Supreme Being[4] all the prisoners were sent down into the courtyard, which we found filled with an enormous quantity of branches and leaves. I pretended to work upon them for a few minutes, and then I withdrew into my own room; several of our wretched companions worked away zealously, and even offered to plant a liberty-pole in the middle of the courtyard. The keeper, less absurd than they, forbade it, saying that such a decoration would not suit a prison. They danced in the court; the jailers attended this strange festival,—it was the day of Pentecost, on which Robespierre permitted God to be adored provided He should not be called by that name. One of them praised me very much (he was not very bad), and said that he thought I would carry myself very well going to the guillotine; I answered him coolly that I hoped I should. Another boasted of the rapidity with which the Revolutionary tribunal got through with its trials; and he added that in order to set things right, it would be necessary to cut off seven thousand heads. One day as I was sitting alone in my room two gendarmes entered; I thought that my last moment of life had come. They questioned me about my father and my brothers; and as the conversation progressed, I hoped that the mere curiosity to see a person of my rank destined for the scaffold had attracted them. They went away, and I was much relieved by their departure. A little while after, a female who had the appearance of a woman of ill-fame came to tell me that she had been ordered by the keeper to lodge in my room, and that she was going immediately to bring in her bed. For a moment I felt extremely irritated, but I restrained myself. I told her that I would leave the room and she could have it all to herself. The women and young girls who were poor had entered into a speculation which I now found useful: they took possession of very small cells, and for money gave them up to other people, finding some way of crowding in elsewhere. I thought of one occupied by the daughter of the Prince of Condé's groom, and she let me have it for a louis in *assignats*; she boasted a great deal of her kindness to me, and indeed it was very fortunate for me. I regretted my fireplace very much on account of its convenience for my neighbours; moreover, it was both inconvenient and dangerous to light fires in open braziers in so narrow a space, though under the circumstances it was absolutely necessary. My new lodging possessed one advantage over those of Madame de la Fayette, in that I could put a chair between my bed and the wall. I could without rising lift the latch of my door, and even look out into the court. My prison life taught me that even the smallest power is precious. The difficulty of procuring light and fire enabled me to succeed in striking a light with steel. I carefully concealed the possession of this treasure, fearing that it might be regarded as a dangerous weapon in a Revolutionary arsenal. The keeper, learning that his name had been used in order to turn me out of my apartment, came to tell me that he had had nothing to do with that enterprise, and requested me to denounce the woman who had contrived it. I replied that I had such a horror of denunciations that I would not give her name. He then proposed that I should return to my room, but I refused to do so; the prison was getting so full that I feared I should be compelled to receive some one into it. Convoys were constantly arriving from the different Departments. One came containing eighty peasant women from the Vivarais, who wore very singular costumes. We questioned them concerning the cause of their arrest; they explained to us in their patois that it was because they went to mass. This was considered so enormous a crime that they were put in the building belonging to the tribunal which was called by our wags Fouquier's shop. Some ladies from Normandy came to our prison. They seemed countrified, though they did not wear their local costumes; they spent their time from morning to night writing memoirs and petitions,—a very dangerous habit during the Reign of Terror, and one which was likely to hasten the hour of death.

I received a letter from my father which made my heart ache. I always awaited and read his letters with deep emotion. He told me that Madame Latour, who was their only consolation, who lightened the burden of their old age, had just been taken away from them; that she had been forced to leave the prison in spite of the efforts she had made to remain or be allowed to return. She begged for imprisonment as earnestly as one usually does for liberty.

All this caused me great grief. I felt more keenly than ever how much my parents needed me, and I again sent in applications to be allowed to go to them; they were fruitless. Fortunately they had with them my sister-in-law, the wife of Louis, Vicomte de Noailles, whom they valued as she deserved; but as she was obliged to take care of Madame d'Ayen, her mother, and Madame la Maréchale de Noailles, her grandmother, who were lodging with her, she could not do very much for my parents. Consequently they were left entirely alone, my father then eighty and my mother sixty.[5] Their forlorn situation was constantly before my mind. One day as I was intensely occupied with thoughts of them, I heard a great noise in the courtyard; I looked out, and saw a convoy enter containing a hundred and fourteen persons from Neuilly-sur-Seine. They had been compelled to pass by the camp of Robespierre's disciples, who had shouted terrible threats at them. As they had received no orders to kill the prisoners, they contented themselves with overwhelming them with threats and insults. The convoy was composed of a great many nobles who had established themselves in the village of Neuilly on account of the *lettres de passe*. (A decree had compelled all nobles who were not imprisoned in Paris to go away several leagues from the city.) A most strange thing to happen at such a time was, that some persons who were not of noble blood, but who wished to be considered so, obeyed this decree, which had no reference to them at all. The servants of the nobles had been arrested with them; and with them were also people of all conditions, among them six nuns of the Visitation,—one of whom was Madame de Croï, sister of Madame de Tourzel. All of these unfortunate creatures were left a whole day in the 'mouse-trap.' I learned that Madame de Choiseul, the mother, Madame Hippolyte de Choiseul, and Madame de Sérent were also of the party. The whole company were searched in the strictest manner. At last, at seven o'clock in the evening, they were put into lodgings. The nuns, to their dismay, were put on the sixth floor, with twenty-five persons; and to make them more wretched, they were put with the lowest creatures. All belonging to this convoy suffered extremely from hunger. We gave them what we could. I remember that I made for Mesdames de Choiseul a panado which they thought delicious. Bread and wine were usually all that was allowed to be offered to the new-comers. This is a minute detail, and is intended to show the destitution which existed in our prison. I have seen poor women, brought from the suburbs of Paris, sleeping on the tables in the refectory. The greatest attention we could bestow upon people was to give up our mattresses to them while they were waiting for theirs.

All those composing the convoy from Neuilly, though scarcely settled in lodgings, came very near being sent in a body to the Conciergerie to perish the next day. About midnight I heard the sound of carriages,—a not uncommon thing, as I slept lightly. A melancholy curiosity, inspired by fear, induced me to rise and see what was going on.

I saw by the light of a number of torches a great many gendarmes and bailiffs, and at the same moment a frightful noise was heard in our corridor. Loud voices cried, 'Let all who belong to the convoy from Neuilly prepare to depart.' I trembled all over, and went out to go and see my neighbours, who, little accustomed to the rules of the house, were quite undisturbed, since they had been told that this was only a removal. I do not remember whether I told them of the fate which immediately threatened them, so they might prepare for it, or whether I left them in ignorance of their death-summons. For some time they remained in suspense; then the jailers came to say that there was a mistake. We afterward learned that it was by mistake that they had come that night to the Plessis. The executioners did not let their wagons remain empty, but went to another prison to fill them. It was necessary to have a certain number of victims every day, except from our prison, where the number varied. I have known as many as sixty-four to be sent from us in one day.

One thing seems almost incredible unless one witnessed it: it is that constantly one could hear the prisoners playing on different instruments, and singing in chorus the Republican airs; and again, that one could see women caring for their dress, and even coquettish, while, besides the guillotine, they were threatened with death by fire and water. We heard that we were to be shot as the Lyonnais were, against a wall which was newly erected in our courtyard and was destined, it was said, for that purpose. In addition to these rumours, the fire in the library of the abbey of St. Germain,—which we saw very plainly,—as well as the explosion of the magazine at Grenelle, gave us a great deal of anxiety. As far as I myself was concerned, I am sure these two events disturbed me but little; but I was terribly anxious on account of those dear to me. The walk in the open air, which was necessary for our existence, became almost intolerable. One day when I was out, I saw several persons dismount who came from Angoumois. It was about six o'clock in the evening; the name of one of them, an old lady named De Boursac, reminded me of two of the king's equerries who bore the same name, and I gave her some information concerning them which seemed to afford her great pleasure. She told me they were her children, and that she had two others with her. My first conversation was a last farewell, for she was executed with them the next day. The pretext of conspiracies began to be fashionable in order to cause the death of a great many persons of different classes at the same time. I comforted myself sometimes with the hope that my parents' advanced age and their virtues would save them, and that I only would perish; for I saw clearly from all the refusals I had received that I should be obliged to renounce entirely the happiness of joining them. This was for me the greatest possible sorrow, but each day brought others. I could never have endured my situation with fortitude had I not resigned myself entirely to the will of God. The charity which we were so frequently called upon to exercise helped to distract our minds. One day, for instance, I met a poor woman who arrived overcome with fatigue from her long, miserable journey, having slept by the way only in infected prisons. The jailer, in order to force her to go to her apartment, which was very high up, spoke to her in most abusive language, and even kicked her, to rouse her from the prostration which overcame her as she mounted the stairs. I begged this cruel citizen not to treat her as a beast of burden, but to put her in my charge. I had great trouble to gain this favour from him, but succeeded with the help of one of my companions in getting her away from the barbarian. I think she was Madame de Richelieu.

Madame de Rochechouart, her mother, was a singular example of the well established fact that prison life cured several very great invalids. When she was arrested at Courteille she was spitting blood so constantly that it was thought she would never reach Paris. On reaching Plessis her health became much better, though she lived in a room where the plaster was still fresh, without fire, and exposed to every wind. I believe it was the strict diet forced upon us by the poor food which produced this happy effect. One ate only what was just necessary to sustain life. The mind was so agitated that the body felt the effects of the strain. I remember that one night I was so hungry that I got up to get some chocolate, wondering that a physical need could distract me from the sad thoughts which beset me when awake. One day I spoke to Madame de la Fayette on this subject, saying to her that I could not conceive how, occupied as we were constantly with thoughts of death, and having it continually before us, we could provide for the next day what was needful to preserve our lives. While we were in the refectory we were informed that a poor woman had thrown herself out of the only window without a grating in the whole house, and that she was dying in the courtyard; it was surely despair which had urged her to this act of folly. I ran to the spot where they had carried her, and found her crushed, and showing no signs of consciousness. The keeper was beside himself, fearing lest this accident should compromise him, and never thought of doing anything for the unfortunate creature. I implored him, as our surgeon had made his rounds and lived at a great distance, to send for one of the physicians who were imprisoned in the building used as a court. He granted my request very unwillingly; and the officers from the hospital could scarcely be induced to come to see the injured woman, as they said it was the duty of the surgeon of the house to attend to her. They found she had no money, and made no attempt to do anything for her. I was extremely irritated at this. My companions in misfortune shared my desire to be of some assistance. I enter into these details only to show that deeds of kindness were the only distraction from our own sufferings.

I always waited with impatience, mingled with fear, the notes that came to me from the Luxembourg. I received one on the morning of June 26. My father wrote me (I transcribe the note): 'Your mother is suffering from severe indigestion, brought on by eating salad, which is all she has for supper; at first I treated her myself, and afterward our neighbours rendered her all sorts of services. We have a good physician here among the prisoners; he has given her two grains of an emetic which have done her much good. She will be able to take liquids to-morrow, and is improving rapidly. You shall hear from her to-morrow. Our tenderest love and kisses, my dear daughter.'

On reading this my heart ached; I thought of my mother as suffering from something like apoplexy, of my father as heart-broken, while I was utterly powerless to help them. I spent the whole day and night in great agitation, and it seemed so long before the sun rose! I went down and sent message after message to the clerk. Finally, when the time when we usually received letters had passed without my getting one, as a great many of our prisoners had husbands at the Luxembourg I went to inquire if they had had their letters; some said no, others manifested a sort of embarrassment which seemed like compassion. I was struck by it, and a suspicion of the calamity with which I was threatened immediately flashed across my mind. I talked of it the whole evening to Madame de la Fayette and other persons. Their terrified expression confirmed my suspicions. I said to them, with extreme emotion: 'You are hiding from me to-day what I shall learn to-morrow. I know what you wish to keep from me. My cousin, you must tell me the dreadful news.'

Accordingly she came into my room early in the morning, and I no longer doubted what my misfortune was. I read the whole story in her face. She did not tell me of the death of both at once; she waited awhile before telling me of the other. I can never express the grief I felt,—the horror of thinking of such virtue, perfect charity, and honour upon the scaffold! My parents' goodness to me, their tenderness, the immense force of their examples, the lessons they taught me,—all came to my mind. My sobs choked me. It was the day before the fast of Saint Peter. I observed it strictly, swallowing only my tears; it is impossible to describe what one feels under such circumstances. I could learn no details, except that they had been beheaded as conspirators. I did not go down-stairs for several days, and it was some time before I went to walk in the courtyard. My neighbours showed me every attention. From that time the thought of death was always before me,—everything recalled it to my mind; and this perhaps soothed the violence of my grief. One of the first visits I made was to a lady who had on the same day lost her husband and her only son, a youth of sixteen. I was told that I might perhaps comfort her; and I tried to do so as well as I could. I continually repeated the prayers for the dying for others and for myself; I repeated them so frequently that I knew them by heart. I felt sorry to end my life without spiritual aid. This was all the sadder since there were two hundred priests in our house; but they were absolutely forbidden to hold any communication with us. Some persons were in despair on this account. I told them that when it was impossible to confess, one should make a sacrifice of one's life and arouse oneself to perfect contrition, and one would obtain pardon. I was not greatly disturbed, because I felt entirely resigned to the will of God.

Three peasant women from Berry, who slept just back of my bed, received their indictments just as they were going to bed. One of them had spit upon a patriot's cloak; another had stepped upon the arm of a statue of Liberty, which had tumbled down; I do not know the crime of the third. They were in a terrible state all night. Their sobbing prevented my sleeping at all. I got up and endeavoured to encourage them, and exhort them to submit to the decree of Providence. After a while they grew more calm, appeared before the tribunal, and were acquitted. This was for the purpose of making it appear that the decisions were rendered with some sort of equity.

These pretended conspiracies multiplied in a frightful manner. After that of the Luxembourg, one was invented at St. Lazare, and another at Bicêtre. The victims collected at the last mentioned prison, as a *dépôt*, were brought to ours, and kept there twenty-four hours. The convoy was escorted by forty gendarmes, armed with guns. There were a good many priests. These unfortunate beings were chained together by twos and threes, like wild beasts; most of them held their breviaries in their hands. All of them were put in the dungeon to sleep, and they were taken away in a body the next day to the Conciergerie. It is even doubted whether they were ever condemned before being beheaded. I cannot explain the barbarous curiosity which incited us to go to the windows to see these itinerant hearses come and go. I remarked one day to some of my companions that under the old régime, we should have gone a long way to avoid meeting a criminal who was going to be hanged, and now we gazed upon every innocent victim. I think we grew somewhat hardened from constant contact with those who were so. The famous Osselin, author of all the decrees against the *émigrés*, was in the party from Bicêtre; he had concealed a dagger under his coat with which he wounded himself several times during the night he passed at the Plessis. These wounds were dressed as well as was possible, and he was carried to the tribunal on a litter. He was guillotined the next day. The sight of this man's suffering, criminal though he was, inspired me with horror beyond description. He was literally cut to pieces.

On the 22d of July it was rumoured in the prison that some of the ladies of the house of Noailles had been condemned. I did not speak of it to Madame de la Fayette, but tried in vain to learn the truth of the report. A little while after, however, I read in a newspaper that Madame la Maréchale de Noailles and Madame la Duchesse d'Ayen had been guillotined. Nothing was said about my dear little sister-in-law.[6] The difficulty of procuring news from outside was extremely great. The servants of the Reign of Terror even trembled for themselves. When I questioned them, they answered vaguely. I no longer doubted the truth of this new calamity; but I wanted to be sure of it before announcing it to Madame de la Fayette, whose fears I sought in vain to arouse, and who was always hoping for the best. At last I paid a jailer to gain for me the confirmation of what I feared.

It was a sorrow to me the whole time I was hiding it from my cousin, and my spirit was crushed. I loved the Vicomtesse de Noailles as a daughter and friend. She possessed every possible virtue and charm, and was the member of my family whom I most loved and confided in.

To find myself bereaved of five members of my family within so short a space of time seemed almost incredible. And how could I tell Madame de la Fayette that she no longer had mother or grandmother or sister! At last she became conscious of the embarrassed manner of those whom she questioned. She asked me the reason; and I answered her by a flood of tears. It was a sad service which I rendered in return for what she had done for me, under the same circumstances. She comprehended the death of her parent and grandparent, but she could not be persuaded of the death of the angel sister whom she adored. I shared all her sorrow, and our hearts bled for each other. Her situation was terrible, and awakened anew my still fresh grief. We frequently talked together of our revered parents; and we were only roused from our stunned condition by misfortunes more recent than our own, which urged us to comfort those who were suffering from them. The indispensable duty of preparing food is a real, though wretched, distraction when the heart is aching.

We were now threatened with a domiciliary visitation; the keeper, who was quite kind to me, advised me to put my devotional books where they would not be seen. I concealed them carefully, as well as my *assignats*, a few of which still remained, between the beams of our cells. This visitation did not take place. One night (I do not exactly remember the date) I heard a great noise of horses' feet; the great gate opened and shut every moment, and horsemen came in and out. At daybreak I found the courtyard filled with gendarmes. They went away without doing anything, and I have never learned why they came.

I had some business to transact with Haly, and we talked afterward of what was going on; and he informed me that soon all persons of my rank were to be beheaded. I realized that I had but little time to live, and profited by the conversation. I set a strict watch over myself, and prayed God to sustain my courage,—a prayer which was fully granted me.

I did not think it necessary to overwhelm my companions with the weight of my griefs and fears. Some of them deluded themselves as certain sick persons do during epidemics, though already attacked by the disease, saying, 'He who just died had a hemorrhage; I have not. The other complained of a pain in his back; I have not felt anything of the sort.' Just so with the prisoners; they said to each other, 'Those who were beheaded were in correspondence with the *émigrés*, they were aristocrats, money was found on their persons,' etc. They tried to persuade themselves that they were not in the category of those who were every day being condemned. I looked at the situation in a different light; it appeared to me impossible, if the Reign of Terror continued, that any one of our class should escape. I felt sure I should suffer the same fate as my parents; I sought to imitate their resignation, and to honour their memory by dying in a manner worthy of them. I thought that terrible armchair[7] had been honoured by the many virtuous persons who had occupied it. Every evening when I went to bed I repeated my *In manus*. I arranged for the distribution of all my small supply of furniture among my companions. I constantly strove to forgive injuries. My parents, who had been very admirable in this respect, were my models. How beautiful, how Christian, how truly worthy of emulation it is to feel no resentment against those who, after having overwhelmed us with insult, conduct us to the tomb in a manner so atrocious! It is only by following the teaching of the Gospel in every respect that one can be enabled to practise a charity so perfect.

One more sacrifice remained for me to make,—the saddest of all: it was, never to see my son again. I can never express what I felt then, or what an effort it cost me to be resigned to it. I believed that God would pardon me; and I was in as peaceful a state of mind as could be expected under such cruel circumstances. I resolved that when I should be called before the tribunal I would make no answer to the questions of the iniquitous judges, but after hearing my sentence read, I would say, 'You are condemning an innocent person; as a Christian I forgive you, but the God of vengeance will judge you.'

I grieved to think that I was not to die for the faith. Ah! how delightful, when one finds one's last hour approaching, to be able to be sure of possessing a crown of glory and dwelling in that country of which Saint Augustine says that 'Truth is the King, Charity the Law, and the Duration, Eternity.' The idea that I was to die only because of the ineradicable stain of aristocracy displeased me inexpressibly.

On the 8th Thermidor, July 27th, 1794, we perceived toward evening an extreme degree of the usual terrible watchfulness. The prisoners were not allowed to go into the courtyard; the gratings were closed. One would have been anxious under any circumstances; but when one is daily expecting one's fate, one has no other fear. I had still, however, a great dread of being killed by piecemeal, as was done on the 2d of September, with pikes, bayonets, and such infernal weapons. I slept as usual; and the next day, the 9th Thermidor, the sound of cannon was heard. The keeper and jailer were in a state of great excitement; their eyes looked haggard and their faces downcast. We knew nothing of what was passing, but we presumed it must be something frightful. That evening their countenances seemed more human, and there was a rumour of the death of Robespierre.

The next day, the 10th, the inhabitants of houses adjoining the Plessis made from their windows signs of satisfaction. Our keepers appeared more serene. We heard cries of joy and clapping of hands in the courtyard; a man named Lafond, who had been in close confinement for five months, and of whose very existence we had been ignorant, had been set at liberty. This was the dawn of less terrible days for us. We believed for the first time that we might possibly be released from our tomb. On the 11th, Madame Rovère's waiting-woman was set at liberty. The moment a prisoner approached the grating, cries of 'Liberty' resounded through the prison; and this word sounded very sweet to our ears. I could not imagine what was going on outside. We learned that the famous Terrorists continued to take the lead in the Convention, that the terrible Collot d'Herbois, who had had us imprisoned, was one of the number, which made me think that people of our class in society would still be imprisoned. The thought of death never left me nor my companions. Madame de Pons was very anxious to leave the Plessis; she obtained permission to go to a private hospital. (The private hospitals were the prisons where prisoners were best lodged and fed.) It was proposed that I should send in the same petition; but I refused to do so for two reasons: first, because I did not wish to act contrary to the will of Providence, which had placed me in the Plessis; and second, because it was very expensive living in the private hospitals.

The men were now allowed to walk in the courtyard with the women; I was disgusted at this. One can easily imagine the unpleasantness of such a mingling of hussars, spies, women and girls of the street. I advised the good nuns not to appear. It was a horrid sight for any decent person, still more for a holy Carmelite. I lent my chamber to these good women that they might say their prayers in peace. One of them told me she could not endure the language of the vulgar creatures who were lodged with her; I told her her only resource was to stop her ears, since she could not alter their conversation. Another went quite out of her mind because she was not set free. One of her companions came for me to quiet her. I went to her and undertook to treat her as though she were ill, persuaded her to take something to drink, and comforted her with the hope of liberty, and after a while she became calm. It was terrible to see her.

As the number of persons who were set at liberty increased every day, we began to hope for escape from our bars, which up to this time we had expected to see open only for us to pass to the scaffold. The women of the lower classes were favoured first; and six months elapsed before any one dared say a word for one of the nobility. I felt real gratification when I saw Monsieur Legendre, the registrar of Mouchy, go out. Every time I had seen him, I had said to myself, 'He is one of the victims of our family; 'and I had felt quite heart-sick on account of it.

Our seclusion was so strict that when I met two men (the men were never allowed to enter the building appropriated to the women) on my corridor it astonished me greatly. They seemed curious, and asked questions. I inquired about these new people, and was told that they were attached to the Committee of General Security, and had considerable influence there. One of them asked me if I belonged to the nobility; I replied that I did. One of my companions reproved me for this, considering it an imprudence. I told her that I never kept back the truth, and besides it would be perfectly useless to do so. These men returned for several days following; they showed a desire to gain the confidence of the prisoners in order to interfere in their affairs. Those who were set at liberty were now frequently of a higher class. Among them were priests, soldiers, and land owners. We had very miserable recruits in their places,—some Terrorists, and a legion of spies. The judges of the Revolutionary tribunal came again to the clerk of our prison to inquire for accused prisoners, who were given permission to go and confer with their defending counsel. As for us, being only suspected, we had no right to do so; but we pretended to have, so as to hear something from those who were dear to us. The first person who came to see me was Madame de la Motte; and the first who succeeded in sending me a letter at this still most dangerous period was the Vicomtesse de Durfort. She offered me her aid and money. I shall never forget this great kindness. Madame de Grimaldi, her mother's sister, who was with us the day she set out for the tribunal, saw Mademoiselle de Pons as she was getting into Fouquier's wagon; she pressed her hand as she bade her good-by, and said, 'I am content; my troubles will soon be over.'

Monsieur Noël inquired for me at the clerk's office; and I was very glad to be able to show my gratitude to him for the proofs of affection he had shown my parents. He proposed to make application for me to be set at liberty. I refused to allow him to do so, urging as my objection that I had read in one of the newspapers a denunciation against Lecointre, of Versailles, issued by the Convention on account of his having secured the release of Madame d'Adhémar from La Bourbe (the convent of Port-Royal, on the Rue de la Bourbe, had been converted into a prison under the appropriate name of Port-Libre), which made me fear to compromise those who took an interest in me and our class generally; and I determined to wait patiently a while longer. Next, the entire convoy from Neuilly was set at liberty amid the cheers of the prisoners. The nobles were not excluded from this measure,—a fact which made me really believe, for the first time, that I should not remain forever in the Plessis; and I wrote to Monsieur Noël that he might bear me in mind. He had sent me tidings of all the members of my family except my son, of whom I could learn nothing; the children of my unfortunate sister-in-law came to see me.[8] Others were present; and I could not utter a single word, so great was my emotion. I embraced them and then retired to my chamber, completely overwhelmed by the heart-rending memories awakened by their presence.

There was now great excitement among the prisoners. When one has no hope, there is nothing to do but to be resigned; but we had laid aside the thought of approaching death and had conceived the idea of being released from captivity.

One day as I was sitting in my old room with the fireplace, which had been vacated, and the possession of which once more was a real pleasure to me, I saw a man come in from outside who was named Fortin; he told me he was a lawyer frequently employed by Monsieur Legendre, a deputy from Paris, and member of the Committee of General Security, and that he could be of service to me. He asked me a great many questions, and inspired me with confidence; he came to see me for several successive days, and asked me for my papers. I showed him proofs that I had never emigrated; that I had not gone outside of the Departments of Paris and the Oise, from which I had certificates of civism and residence; that I was imprisoned only as a noble, and that there was not the slightest accusation against me. I afterward entered into correspondence with him.

Letters circulated more freely; and we could send them out by the prisoners, who were leaving every day. I commissioned the governess of Madame de Chauvelin's children to carry tidings of me to my mother-in-law. We had learned that deputies had been sent into all the prisons to release the prisoners, and that Bourdon, of the Oise, and Legendre had charge of ours.

On the 16th of October, 1794, the great gate opened, and we saw the carriage of these deputies enter,—which seemed a strange and pleasant sight, since hitherto whenever a vehicle entered the courtyard it departed loaded with victims. The deputies ascended to the clerk's office, where the prisoners of the lower class were called up. Eighty of them were at once set at liberty. The nobles were still ignorant whether or not they would soon be numbered among the elect. The deputies adjourned their second sitting to October 18. I felt that this would probably be the day on which we would be subjected to our examinations, and I dreaded it on account of my love of the truth. I feared that I might be unfaithful to it, or that if I spoke the truth plainly I might remain several years more in captivity. As I was turning these thoughts over in my mind, which was very much troubled (it was the famous 18th of October), I received orders to present myself at the clerk's office. As we entered the room where the deputies were, they said to us in a severe tone: 'Let the *ci-devants* leave the room; it is not proper to examine the good *sans-culottes* in their presence.' We retired and waited almost three hours, most of the time standing. I conversed all this time with Madame de la Fayette. At last my turn came. Bourdon asked me my names; I told them to him. He jumped up out of his chair and exclaimed, 'These are terrible names! We cannot set this woman at liberty; her case must be carried before the Committee of General Security.'

I silently implored the aid of Heaven to enable me to watch over myself at this moment and not to violate the truth.

Bourdon asked me several insignificant questions with regard to my abode, the time of my imprisonment, etc. Legendre, whom Fortin and Monsieur Noël had interested in my behalf, assumed a kindly manner, and pointed out to his colleague that 'my papers were good, that I had been spoken well of to him, that he knew that I had been a member of the charitable board of St. Sulpice.' I felt a real satisfaction in being under obligations to the poor. Fortin asked me what I had done to aid the Revolution. I replied, 'All my life I have done any kind act that I could; and I gave money to poor volunteers on my father's estate when they set out for the army.' A prisoner who was present at my examination had the kindness to bestow a panegyric upon me which the keeper approved and added to, praising my submission to the rules of the house.

I leaned quietly upon a table on which were all the judges' papers. I learned afterward that my manner was considered haughty. No sentence was pronounced upon me, and at last I told them that the unparalleled miseries I had endured gave me a right to justice from them. Legendre seemed somewhat moved, but I went out of his presence a moment after feeling that my cause was lost. He treated Madame de la Fayette in a most insulting manner. He told her 'that he had great fault to find with her, that he detested her husband, herself, and her name.' She replied with equal courage and nobleness 'that she would always defend her husband and that a name was not a crime.'

Bourdon asked her several questions, to which she replied with firmness. Legendre finally ended this pleasant dialogue by telling her that she was an insolent creature. They decided to liberate the greater part of our companions. I retired fully persuaded that I should be again entered in the jail-book. But one of my neighbours assured me that I was on the list of those who were to be set at liberty. I received on this occasion strong proofs of the interest my companions took in my doubtful fate; I returned to my own room sure that I was to resume my fetters; I was resigned to this, as was also Madame de la Fayette. It is not nearly so hard to feel so when one has experienced many misfortunes, and when one has no hope of being restored to those one loves.

I have noticed that it is better, when one is about to give up life, not to be surrounded by those who make it so dear. What one suffers for others and on one's own account is, taken together, too much to be endured.

On the 19th of October, 1794, at ten o'clock in the morning, while I was busy with my morning duties, I heard my door open suddenly. A little while before I should have been sure that it was the announcement of my death, and I did not even now think this sudden interruption brought me good news; but some one, whose name I do not remember, said to me delightedly, 'You are free!' My heart, so unused to pleasurable emotions, was slow to entertain the idea. The keeper entered, confirmed the news, and brought me my *acte de liberté*. I then thought sadly of how little use it would be to me. Deprived of every comfort, separated from my son and my parents, from Madame de Chimay,—the only friend that Heaven had left to me,—without a home, and in want of the very necessaries of life, I felt irritated by the congratulations of the jailers and the gendarmes who had formerly threatened me with the guillotine, and was very much afraid that they would, according to their usual custom, manifest their feelings by embracing me; but I fortunately escaped. In this confused condition of thought and feeling, the memory of my dear son and the thought of what I could be to him aroused my courage, which had succumbed at this terrible crisis. It was necessary to pack up my small wardrobe, which took only a short time. All my effects were put in two bundles. I bade farewell to Madame de la Fayette, who, with several other persons, was destined to remain in prison. I felt very grateful for the pleasure which, despite her unfortunate situation, she showed at seeing me released from bondage. I engaged a commissioner at the grating, who helped me with my baggage. We arrived safely at the house of my mother-in-law, who then lived on the Rue de Bellechasse. She received me most kindly and tenderly. I found her with my niece; they did not expect me, and neither did Monsieur Noël, who had on account of his interest and attachment for me laboured to have me liberated. He came to see me, and assured me that Madame Drulh (a former governess of Madame de Mailly) was very anxious to have me stay at her house. I accepted the kind offer for a few days, though I feared to compromise her, since there was still great ill-feeling entertained against our class. I went to see my nurse, Royale, who was much moved at sight of me; she had saved all she could for me. I asked her for some mourning dresses, as I had not worn any since the death of my parents. Madame Latour came to see me. Our interview was interrupted by bitter weeping. It is impossible to imagine what I felt at seeing the person who had last seen my parents, and who had shown them such true affection; it carried me back to the first hours of my bereavement. She thought me frightfully changed; I looked ten years older, and like one risen from the dead. A few of the servants of our house also came to see me. The number of those who were faithful was very small, the Revolution having made a portion of them 'patriots,' and some of them even Terrorists.

It was a great pleasure to me to see my old friends once more,—among others, Madame de Tourzel, who had gone through more terrible scenes than any of them; she had made the fearful journey from Varennes, had been sentenced by the 'bloody tribunal' of the 2d of September, and had been six times imprisoned. I could scarcely believe my eyes as I embraced her. She showed under all the trying circumstances in which she was placed a courage beyond all praise. It was really pitiful, after the solemn scenes in which we had been actors and witnesses, to see the value we attached to the small necessities of life after having been so long deprived of them. It was an intense pleasure to me to be able to use a knife, a clean plate, scissors, to look in a mirror, etc.; but the greatest delight of all was to be no longer subjected to the low and wicked. I feel some gratitude, however, to Haly, the keeper, and Tavernier, the clerk, for having preserved and restored to me the clock I mentioned before, which I valued very much.

The deliverance from all my past ills was very pleasant to me, but a pall seemed over everything; I felt a distaste for everything, as one does for medicines. Accustomed as I had been to be surrounded by sympathizing love, the thought of my isolation overwhelmed me. It seemed that though the period of my misfortune was becoming more remote, liberty increased the intensity of my feelings; and my thoughts grew sadder every day. The thought of death necessarily most effectually blunts the edge of grief, since it brings us near to the moment when we find what we have lost, and we cease to regret. My mind returned to its former grief with renewed constancy, and I could no longer open my heart to my friends. I was not sure that my son was alive until I had been a long time out of prison. I had planned to retire to a village, with one servant, and there mourn for my loved ones. The consolation of rendering to the precious remains of my parents the duties observed in all ages, and by all religions, was refused me. Their ashes are mingled with those of criminals in the cemetery of Picpus, the ground of which has been bought by Madame la Princesse de Hohenzollern, sister of the Prince of Salm-Kirbourg. But at the last great day when all hearts shall be opened, God will know how to recognize his elect, and show them, resplendent in glory, to the assembled nations.

I was one of the first, after the re-establishment of the church, to have prayers said for my parents. A Mass was said for them at the Foreign Missions. We have need of their protection. I trust that their heavenly blessing may rest upon their children and grandchildren to the latest generation.

The forlorn situation of my mother-in-law, who, though she had not been in prison, had been under arrest in her own house with a dozen jailers, who never left her until their pay failed, determined me to devote myself to taking care of her; but I could not do this as the law exiling nobles was not abrogated. We were allowed only two *décadis*[9] to make our preparations, and immediately after were to retire some leagues from Paris. It was necessary for me to seek some shelter; Madame de la Rochefoucauld-Doudeauville, a relative of mine, proposed to me to come to her house in the country, and assured me that I was welcome to anything she had. Her kind feeling for me caused her to offer what she really had not; for the little house which she occupied in the village of Wisson, near Longjumeau, was scarcely large enough for her own family. I went to see it, and concluded to rent some lodgings near her and Mesdames de la Suze and de la Roche-Aymon. I did not, however, have the opportunity to occupy them, as I obtained a prolongation of my sojourn in Paris, and during that time the law was repealed.

After remaining six months at the house of good Madame Drulh, I found a vacant room in the house where my mother-in-law was staying, which I took immediately. It was extremely cold, and the winters of 1794 and 1795 were very trying. I had no one to wait upon me. I would come in to go to bed, and find the fire had gone out, and this frequently after having walked a long distance. I missed much of the sunlight in the streets as I had to prepare both my breakfast and my supper. In order to attend Mass I had to go out before day and resort to the secret places of worship, where pious mechanics gladly received me. There was nothing more edifying during the whole Reign of Terror than the courage they showed in procuring for the faithful the opportunities of engaging in the exercise of their religion. I dressed myself as a servant, and consequently could not wear any of the warm *crêpes* which luxury supplies for us; this masquerade was necessary in order not to make known the places where the holy mysteries were celebrated.

On Christmas day, 1794, when the Réaumur thermometer fell to eighteen degrees, I sat in the Rue Montorgueil, near Montmartre, through the whole of the office, the sermon, vespers, and the benediction. I found myself on the Pont Neuf at six o'clock in the evening, and the north wind cut my face like a knife. I had formed the habit, after leaving prison, of going out into the streets alone; I continued to do so, and found it very convenient. I never took cold once during that severe winter. I met my old acquaintances from time to time, and always felt deeply moved. We invariably talked about the treatment in the different prisons, and the sufferings we had endured. Almost all the prominent persons had been imprisoned, or at least under arrest in their own houses, which was substituted only as a great favour in the case of the infirm or aged. We found a certain variety in the horrors; but on comparison the Conciergerie and the Plessis proved to have been the most terrible of all the prisons, on account of the treatment and the great number of victims who were constantly taken from them to the scaffold.

Madame Doudeauville very kindly persuaded me to spend a few days with her at her country-house. Her loveliness, the attractions of her home, the sincere sorrow she felt at the death of my parents, and her goodness to me, cheered me somewhat, though I was so overcome with grief. I had almost forgotten how to write an ordinary letter, and had long been entirely out of the habit of doing so. The carelessness of the style of this memoir and its dullness are proof of what I have stated.

At last I received news from my son, and this restored me to life.

The latter part of the winter was terribly hard, on account of both the scarcity of food and the cold. It was almost impossible to procure wood, candles, or bread. We sent thirty and forty leagues, for them. I carried something in my pocket when I went out to dine, even at the house of Madame la Duchesse d'Orleans, who lodged in the Rue de Charonne, near the barrier at the Faubourg St. Antoine. She boasted of having a farmer who sent her a loaf of bread weighing four pounds, every week. She had wretched fare; her dishes were what are commonly called *culs-noirs*. A dwarf served her as butler and valet. She endured her poverty nobly, and joked about it. I remember hearing a lady say to the queen, the wife of Louis XVI., while she was at the Tuileries, that she knew one woman more unfortunate than she, and that was the Duchess of Orleans. She had inherited a hundred and twenty millions from Monsieur le Duc de Penthièvre, of which the nation took possession, and did not even give her enough out of it to support life.

The Revolution has taught us how to understand poverty, by causing us to experience it ourselves. Two farmers on the estate of Mouchy, whose names I record with gratitude,—Duraincy and Isoré,—sent me some flour. I am sure a casket full of gold could never have given me so much pleasure. People conversed in the evening only of what they had eaten during the day. Servants stood in line from three o'clock in the morning trying to procure provisions. Women and young girls often waited twenty-four hours. Sometimes a whole day was spent in obtaining a loaf of bread or two ounces of something made of hempseed, green pears, and all sorts of horrid stuff. Whenever I had any of this unwholesome food I divided it with those about me. It was the *maximum*[10] that reduced Paris to this state of distress.

Soon I found myself in a fresh dilemma, being sent away from my lodgings, which had been rented to some one else. Madame de Tourzel offered me a residence in the name of Madame de Charost, and I accepted it; it was very high up. I dined with my mother-in-law, and consequently, in the evening, was exceedingly weary from the number of steps I had climbed; for I was very much broken down from all I had endured. The charming society of that house amply repaid me for all the fatigue I suffered. My mother-in-law was obliged to leave the house where she was staying, and Madame de Beuvron lent her hers. We had very fine lodgings, but our food was miserable. My mother-in-law and I lived for three francs a day (in *assignats*) at an eating-house,—the uncertainty of the future compelling me to economize the small means still left me. Both the quantity and quality of the food was insufficient; nothing could be more disgusting than the meats which were served us. I had long been accustomed to such fare; but I grieved on my mother-in-law's account, though she never complained of it. She endured the horrors of her situation with admirable resignation and patience. Heaven doubtless sustained her to the end of her sad life. A most fortunate thing for me now happened: Madame de Beuvron went to occupy her own house, and several apartments became vacant in that of Madame de la Rochefoucauld; we took possession of them on the 1st of October, 1795. This arrangement was very much more agreeable for me; I have continued to live there ever since, and I desire nothing better. Being near my son and daughter-in-law adds another attraction to it; and as my life now passes in the most commonplace fashion I end this tiresome story, asking the reader to excuse its faults.

PARIS, February 11, 1804.

(Signed)

NOAILLES DE DURFORT-DURAS.

ADDENDA.

On re-reading my memoirs I find a great many repetitions, particularly in the notes where I have several times referred to Madame Latour.

When my honoured father left the prison of the Luxembourg to be removed to the Conciergerie he said in a sorrowful voice to the prisoners who accompanied him to the doorway: 'At sixteen I went into the trenches to serve my king; at eighty I mount the scaffold in obedience to the will of God.'

The 'Messager du Soir,' though an organ of the Reign of Terror, inserted the following article in its columns on the 20th of May, 1795, year III. of the Republic:—

'When the venerable Maréchal de Noailles-Mouchy, who was all his life the father of the unfortunate, was led out with his good wife to be beheaded, a wretch cried aloud: "Now the *'sans-culottes,'* will enjoy your bread and drink your wine." He answered with that serenity which a pure conscience bestows upon an honest man: "God grant that you may have bread for another year, and that you may not be compelled to devour one another."'

DIFFERENT NOTES AND MEMORANDA RELATING TO MONSIEUR AND MADAME DE MOUCHY, AND THEIR DAUGHTER-IN-LAW, LOUISE NOAILLES, WHO WAS CONDEMNED AND EXECUTED THE 4TH THERMIDOR, 22D OF JULY, 1794.

The following was brought to me from the office by Robert Lindet, when I went to the court sitting at the abbey of St. Germain to reclaim the last will and testament of my father and mother, which was then delivered up to me:

National Convention.

Committee of General Security of the National Convention. Fifth day of the third decade of the first month of the French Republic, one and indivisible.

The Committee authorizes Citizen Braut to go to Mouchy, near Beauvais, for the purpose of arresting the citizen Noailles-Mouchy, (whose son, the former Prince de Poix, has emigrated), the wife of the said Mouchy, and all other persons who are suspected; he shall conduct them to the prison of La Grande Force, make all necessary search and requisitions for papers, set seals, and bring away everything that seems suspicious. After the seals have been affixed the citizen Braut, in the virtue of these presents, shall cause the citizen Mouchy, to be arrested wherever he shall be found, and also his wife and other suspected persons. He can moreover call for the assistance of the constitutional authorities and the armed force.

(Signed)

VADIER, PANIS,

LAVICOMTERIE, JAGOT,

DAVID, and DUBARRAT.[11]

Certified to be conformable to the warrant deposited in the clerk's office of the prison of La Force by me the undersigned.

PARIS, 5 Prairial year II.

(Signed)

S. F. RICHELOT, clerk.

EXTRACT FROM THE MINUTES OF THE CLERK'S OFFICE OF THE REVOLUTIONARY TRIBUNAL, ESTABLISHED AT PARIS, MARCH 10, 1793.

By decision rendered the 9th Messidor, year II. of the French Republic, at a public session of the tribunal, composed of: Naulin, vice-president; Bravet, Legarnier, Launay, judges, who signed the minute, together with the clerk, upon the declaration of the jury, setting forth that Phillippe Noailles-Mouchy, and others before mentioned in the said minute are proven to have been the enemies of the people, by having been accomplices of the traitor Capet in the distribution of money employed by that tyrant to bribe refractory priests by whose aid the civil war was fomented; by seconding with all their abilities and means all the projects of the former court to overthrow liberty, crush the people, and re-establish despotism; by holding intercourse with the enemies of the Republic, for the purpose of obtaining men and money to assist in the invasion of French territory; by seeking to promote by speech and writing the degradation and dissolution of the national representation and the re-establishment of the monarchy; by assassinating patriots in the Champ de Mars, as well as by bringing about the civil war, and seeking to excite citizens against one another; and finally, by seeking by every possible means to annihilate public liberty.

It appears that the tribunal, having heard the examination by the public accuser, has, in accordance with the law, condemned to death Phillippe Noailles-Mouchy, aged seventy-nine years, born at Paris, ex-noble, ex-duke, and marshal of France, former governor of the palaces of Versailles, and Marly and of other places, living at Mouchy, in the Department of the Oise, and at Paris in the Rue de l'Université, and declared his property confiscated to the Republic.

From an indictment drawn up by Fouquier, the public accuser, on the 8th Messidor, year II., the following extract has been taken verbatim:—

Noailles-Mouchy, was the agent of Capet for the distribution of sums of money by means of which he bribed refractory priests, *émigrés*, and other accomplices of their infamous intrigues, and paid them to commit their crimes.

Extract conformable to the minute given gratis by me, the keeper of archives.

(Signed)

PERRET.

Copy of the label put upon the inkstand of Monsieur le Maréchal de Mouchy, found among his effects at the Luxembourg, and which has been returned to his relatives:—

No. 20.

Noailles, upon whom the sword of the law

has rendered justice.

DIFFERENT LETTERS AND NOTES FROM MY
SISTER-IN-LAW, WRITTEN FROM THE PRISON
OF THE LUXEMBOURG.

To Monsieur Grelet, her children's tutor, who

was like a father to them.

I confide to the keeping of Monsieur Grelet my three children,—my two boys, and my girl. I declare that it is my most positive and express desire, in case I should come to want, that he should have charge of them. I give over to him all my rights and authority over them. I implore him to be a mother to them, and under no circumstances to allow any one to separate them from him. I authorize him to remove them from one place to another as may seem best to him,—in short, to treat my children as if they were his own. I am sure that all who care for me will most sacredly regard this my desire.

Written in the prison of the Luxembourg, this 24th Messidor, year II. of the French Republic, one and indivisible.

(Signed)

LOUISE NOAILLES, wife of NOAILLES.

Letter of the Same to the Same.

I send you, my dear friend, a short will which I am told will be valid; I keep a copy of it in my pocket. Make the best use you can of it as well as that of my mother, communicating it to the proper persons when the time comes. God has sustained and will sustain me; I have the strongest faith in Him. Farewell, my dear friend; I shall feel grateful to you even in Heaven. Be sure of this. Farewell, Alexis, Alfred, Euphémie. Love God all your lives; cling to Him always. Pray for your father and live for his happiness. Remember your mother, and that her dearest wish for you was that you should be the children of God. I give you all my last blessing. I hope to find you again in the bosom of your Father. I shall not forget our friends, and I hope they will not forget me.

The note enclosed is for Louis. (So she called her husband.) Put it with the one you already have.

(Signed)

L. NOAILLES.

Louise Noailles to her Husband.

You will find a letter from me, my husband, written at different times and very disconnectedly. I should have liked to rewrite it, and to add many things; but that is impossible now. I can therefore only renew the assurance of the love which you already know I bear to you, and which I shall bear with me to my grave. You know what terrible circumstances surround me, and you will be glad to learn that God has cared for me; that he has sustained my strength and my courage; that the hope of gaining, by the sacrifice of my life, the eternal welfare of you and my children will continue to encourage me through the moments most terrible to the flesh. May it please God that this thought may decide you to live for eternity, and to strive in unison with me. I confide to you my dear children, who have been the comfort of my life, and will be, I hope, the comfort of yours. I am sure you will seek to strengthen in them the principles I have inculcated; they are the only source of true happiness and the only means of obtaining it. I have now, my husband, one last request to make,—one which I am sure you will think superfluous when you know what it is. I implore you with my last breath never to separate my dear children from Monsieur Grelet, in whose charge I have left them. I charge my dear Alexis to tell you all we owe to him. There are no kind cares and attentions which he has not shown me, particularly since I have been in prison. He has been both father and mother to these poor children; he has sacrificed himself for them and for me under the most trying circumstances with a tenderness and courage for which we can never be sufficiently grateful. The only comfort I can have is to know that my children are in his charge. You will not disturb this arrangement, my husband; and I am sure you will have a sacred regard for this wish of mine. I do not know what will become of my poor Euphémie, but I declare to you that for a thousand reasons I desire that the Citizeness Thibaut should no longer have the care of her.

My husband, I bid you a last farewell. May we be once more reunited in Eternity.

From the Same to Alexis, her eldest Son,

the 27th Messidor.

I charge you, my dear child, to give your father a detailed account of the obligations we are under to the citizen Grelet. I rely upon your heart to make him understand all he has been to you and to me. Do not forget to say that he wished to share his purse with us, and that we have lived entirely at his expense.

I send you, my dear children, my tenderest love and kisses....

The Same to Monsieur Grelet.

It was not my fault, my dear child [thus she was accustomed to address Monsieur Grelet], that you waited yesterday so long and in vain; I am very sorry for it, and also for all the trouble that this mother and children cause you. Remember that you are the only and blessed comfort that I have in this world. I have not heard from you since the little message you sent as you were going out from breakfast at Citizeness Raymond's till yesterday at half past eleven. It was then too late for my answer to go out. I have told you the condition of my linen. I am in great need of some; get some for me from my confidential servant.

I highly approve of your lodgings; shall I tell my sister-in-law that I insist upon your remaining with your brothers? The letter which you have seems to me more persuasive than anything I could say.

Farewell, my dear children; I love you all four more tenderly than ever.

I am well as usual.

(Signed)

L. Noailles.

Last Letter from Madame de Noailles to

Monsieur Grelet.

I have received, my dear child, all that you sent me; I thank you a thousand times, and shall never cease to repeat, as the poor do, 'God reward you.' This is and ever will be the cry of my heart, from above as well as from here below. I am ashamed of having said yesterday 'this' mother and children. The expression troubles me; I should have said as usual, and I do say now with all my heart, *your* mother and *your* brothers, whom you have specially under your care, because you are the eldest. But for you, my dear child, what would have become of them?

Farewell, dear, dear children; I send you my tenderest love and kisses.

(Signed)

Louise Noailles.

EXTRACT FROM THE LAST WILL AND TESTAMENT OF ANNE-JEANNE-CATHERINE-DOMINIQUE-ADRIENNE-LOUISE-PAULINE NOAILLES, WIFE OF THE FORMER VICOMTE DE NOAILLES.

In the name of the Father, of the Son, and of the Holy Ghost:

I commend my soul to God; I die in the religion of the Roman Catholic Apostolic Church, in which by the mercy of God I was born, and have always lived. My love for this holy religion has grown with my growth; I trust that it will be my support when I come to die, as it has been my strength and comfort during every moment of my life. I believe firmly all that it has pleased God to reveal to us, and all that the Catholic, Apostolic, and Roman Church teaches.

I hope in its promises; I put my whole trust in the merits of Jesus.

I request Monsieur de Noailles, my husband, to undertake the execution of my will; I am glad to give him in this last act of my life a fresh proof of my confidence, and of a love which has made me so happy. I therefore place in his hands all the interests I have of every kind whatever.

I hope he will regard them as his own, and that when he is occupied with the details he will recall her who felt so truly happy in being united to him and all she suffered for her love. I beg him to accept the little bust of Adrien, and the two portraits of our children. I bless these dear children with my latest breath. I implore them for the sake of the love I bear them to draw near to God with all their hearts, to strive to obey His laws. I assure them, by my own experience, that only thus will they be able to taste pure and lasting happiness amid all the changes of this life. I beg them to remember that the desire for their real happiness has been the continual object of my thoughts and prayers, and that I shall never cease to implore God for it if he mercifully receives me. I leave them all the portraits of their father. I charge them to reverence and love him all the days of their lives, and to bring to his remembrance, by their great tenderness, her who gave them birth. I beg them to remember that it is to them I confide the care of his happiness; and I charge them to perform my duty toward him.

I commend myself to the prayers of my relatives and friends, and rely upon them to have prayers said to God for the repose of my soul.

I request the executor of my will (who shall be Monsieur de Grammont in default of my husband) to give to my mother and sisters whatever they may wish of the things which belonged to me.

I give my mother a renewed assurance of my most tender and filial affection. I owe her a great share of the happiness of my life, and especially shall I owe her my eternal happiness if God in his mercy receives me.

I request Madame de la Fayette, in the name of the affection we bear each other, not to give way to grief, but to bear up for the sake of her husband and children. Her real happiness, her interests, and the interests of all who are dear to her will always be mine; and I shall bear them with me forever. I implore her and also my two other sisters to remember that this union which has been the delight and comfort of our lives is not broken up, that we are parted only for a little while, and that we shall be reunited, I hope, for eternity. [Here follow bequests.] I assure my father once more of the true and tender love I have for him; I beg him to remember me, and to believe that as I prayed earnestly and unceasingly for his happiness in this world, so will it be one of my dearest duties to implore the Father for him in another.

Written at Paris, this 5th of April, 1794.

(Signed)

LOUISE NOAILLES.

In the name of the Father, of the Son, and of the Holy Ghost:

Receive, O Lord, the sacrifice of my life; I give my spirit into thy hands. Help me, O my God! Leave me not when my strength fails.

I have always lived, and hope by the grace of God to die, in the Roman Catholic Apostolic religion.

I forgive all my enemies (if I have any) from the bottom of my heart; I pray that God may grant them his fullest pardon.

I request that payment may be made, etc.

Written at Paris, and

(Signed)

LOUISE NOAILLES.

I learned on leaving the prison that there was a certain lady named Lavet who had been at the Conciergerie at the same time as Mesdames de Noailles and d'Ayen. I hastened to go to see her and ask for an account of their short and terrible residence in that prison, which she gave me as follows:—

Mesdames de Noailles and d'Ayen arrived at the Conciergerie on the 21st of July, 1793, excessively fatigued by their removal from the Luxembourg, which had been made in very rough wagons. They were suffering for want of food, which it was impossible to procure for them, as it was nine o'clock at night, and the rules of the prison did not permit anything to be brought in after nightfall. We could only give them some gooseberry water to quench their thirst. They were put into a dungeon where there were three other women, one of whom knew Madame de la Fayette by reputation. She took a kind interest in her neighbours, and undertook to help them to procure beds; but the turnkeys having discovered that they had not so much as forty-five francs,—which sum they exacted for furnishing them,— absolutely refused to supply them. They had been robbed of everything at the Luxembourg; the Vicomtesse de Noailles possessed only fifty sous. Madame Lavet, touched by the situation of this unfortunate family, gave her bed to Madame la Maréchale de Noailles, obtained one for Madame d'Ayen, and proposed to her daughter that she should lie down on a cot. She would not do so, however, saying that she had now too little time to live to make it worth while to take the trouble. Madame d'Ayen spent a greater part of the night trying to persuade her to do so, but could not succeed. The angelic woman borrowed a book of devotions and a light, by means of which she read and prayed to God constantly. She stopped only long enough to wait upon her grandmother, who slept at intervals for several hours. Every time she awakened the grandmother read over her indictment, saying to herself: 'No, it is not possible that I am to die on account of a conspiracy of which I know nothing; I will plead my cause before the judges so that they shall not be able to condemn me.' She thought of her dress, feared it was rumpled, arranged her bonnet, and would not believe it possible that the next day could be the last of her life. Madame d'Ayen had fears, but no conviction of the imminent danger which threatened her. She dozed for a while. She was greatly worried, wishing to send her watch—the only thing she had left—to her children. She urged her companions to take charge of it; but they did not dare to do so. The Vicomtesse de Noailles made the same request with regard to an empty portfolio, a portrait, and some hair; but she received the same reply, that such commissions would compromise them all. She made Madame Lavet promise to tell Monsieur Grelet that she should die in peace and perfect resignation, but that she longed from the bottom of her heart to see him and her children. Some one in that sorrowful room uttered the name of her dear sister, Madame de la Fayette; she forbade them to speak of her lest it should compromise her. Madame de Noailles, the younger, of whom I have just spoken, did not even think of sleeping; her eyes were wide open, contemplating that Heaven which she was so soon to enter. Her face showed the serenity of her soul. Thoughts of eternity sustained her courage. Such calmness was never seen in that terrible place. She forgot herself entirely in caring for her mother and grandmother.

At six o'clock in the morning, in order to distract their minds, we undertook to give them some breakfast. Mesdames de Boufflers brought them some chocolate. They remained with them a few moments and then bade them a final farewell.

Nine o'clock struck; the bailiffs came, and found their victims surrounded by the weeping friends who had known them only twelve hours. The mother made some arrangements in case they should be acquitted. The daughter, who never once doubted the fate which awaited her, thanked Madame Lavet in her sweet, gracious way, expressed her gratitude for all her kindness, and then said: 'I read good fortune in your face; you will not be beheaded.'

This is all that I have been able to learn from Madame Lavet in reference to that terrible scene.

(Signed)

NOAILLES,

Duchesse de Duras.

1. The Prince de Poix, who had defended and followed the king on the 10th of August.

2. A line of Racine.—TRANSLATER.

3. This 'little château,' dated from the sixteenth century, is one of the finest specimens of Renaissance architecture in existence, and was included in the gift of the Duc d'Aumale to the French nation (1886). The Grand Château, where Condé had spent twenty years of his life, and which was so famous for its literary associations with the names of Molière, Boileau, Racine, and La Fontaine, was destroyed in 1793.—TRANSLATER.

4. One of the holidays laid down in the revised Revolutionary calendar.—TRANSLATER.

5. A detailed account of the prison of the Luxembourg may be found in the journal of Madame Latour.

6. The Vicomtesse de Noailles.

7. The victims brought before the Revolutionary tribunal for examination were placed in an armchair, and from it they were taken to the scaffold.

8. Alexis and Alfred de Noailles, sons of the Vicomtesse de Noailles.

9. The division of ten days, by which the Republican calendar supplanted the week—TRANSLATER.

10. The highest price at which food, at that time, was allowed to be sold in Paris.

11. The first Revolutionary tribunal had been established by the law of the 17th of August, 1792.

MADAME LATOUR'S MEMOIR.

CONTAINING AN ACCOUNT OF THE LIFE IN THE
PRISON OF THE LUXEMBOURG, WHERE SHE
WAS IMPRISONED DURING THE YEARS 1793
AND 1794, IN COMPANY WITH MADAME LA
MARÉCHALE DUCHESSE DE MOUCHY.

The last two years, during which I shared the misfortunes of Monsieur and Madame de Mouchy, have abounded in such precious moments to me that in order to preserve the remembrance of them (not for myself,—to me they are ever present,—but for those near to me), I relate as an eye-witness the sad circumstances under which they manifested the nobility of their souls, and the beautiful spirit in which they endured their captivity.

I trust I may be pardoned for speaking of myself frequently when I am talking about them, and for saying 'we' when I ought to say Monsieur and Madame la Maréchale; but I may say that their interests had become mine, that my existence, on account of my attachment to them, depended so much upon theirs, that everything I thought and felt was in common with them. I was very careful in this matter; for they treated me with such distinction that it often embarrassed me. They thought, these honoured friends (may I be pardoned for expressing myself thus), that they were under obligations to me; but they were mistaken. I was never more proud of anything than of waiting upon them in prison. Let no one praise me for it; I do not deserve praise.

Madame de Duras has given in her memoirs an account of the life her honoured parents led at Mouchy. I cannot express the despair in which they were left when she was taken away from them; they refused to take any nourishment. I spent the whole night beside Madame de Mouchy, who did nothing but weep and moan over the loss of her dear daughter, so she always called her. Ten days after her departure a body of about sixty armed men arrived, with some of the municipal authorities and the Commissioners of the Committee of General Security, furnished with an order to search everywhere for a quantity of arms which were said to be concealed in the château, and to arrest any one who should be suspected. They found only one pistol, but seized some title-deeds which the *féodiste*[12] was arranging for the purpose of carrying them to the prescribed place of deposit. The commissioners were in a rage, and had him put in prison.

They treated his wife, who was in a delicate condition, in the most inhuman manner, and took away their badges from the municipal officers, who they declared were in collusion with him. They threatened the whole village, and said they were sorry they had not brought a guillotine and cut off the head of every citizen. They ransacked and almost pulled down some portions of the château. The commissioners demanded to see some lead coffins which were supposed to be in the vault of the chapel. After much searching they found three of these. This capture did not satisfy them; they thought that money had been concealed in the coffins, but they were mistaken in their suspicion. They compelled the municipal authorities, though not in accordance with their duties, to assist in the search. The latter were almost frightened to death.

The consternation in the village was so great that no one dared move out of one's house. The night was even more terrible. The peasants who composed our guard became intoxicated with the wine they found in the cellar, and fired their guns off under the windows of the houses; we thought our last hour had come. At last, after three days of searching, the chief commissioner affixed the seals, seized all the silver,—alleging as a pretext for doing so the fact that some of the dishes had on them armorial bearings,—drew up a *procès-verbal*, and allowed us to pack up only in the presence of the jailers, so that they might see what we carried away with us. They restored the badges to the municipal officers, and concluded to carry the *féodiste* away with them. His wife was left on account of her condition. We were so miserable during the whole of the three days we passed under the conduct of this troop, that, incredible as it may seem, we were anxious to reach the prison to which we were destined. Picture a courtyard filled with the wagons in which we were to be taken away, two large carts loaded with title-deeds, coffins, a clock, some old pictures, trunks, and other things; the remains of the dead scattered about; pieces of wood, loose papers, and other rubbish; the ragged country guardsmen with frightened faces, and one can have some idea of the condition of Mouchy, at the moment of our departure with the chief commissioner, who made us halt at St. Brice long enough for him to make inquiries about a few persons in the vicinity, after which he returned to his carriage content with his discoveries. We talked a good deal as we went along, and found out that they were going to take Monsieur and Madame de Mouchy, to stay for the night at their own house, pretending that it would be impossible to procure even absolute necessities for them at La Force at so late an hour. We reached the Hôtel Mouchy, at two o'clock in the morning.

The commissioner left them there two days, during which time applications were made to the Committee of General Security, who ordered a suspension of the affixing of seals in the house. Janon, the commissioner of the section of Grenelle who was charged with this duty, observed that it was not worth while doing it because there were no proper signatures. He was requested to delay until the signatures could be obtained. Unfortunately the members of the committee had gone to dinner, and would not reassemble till the evening; then our commissioner (a man named Braut) would listen to no further entreaties, and declared that he had done wrong not to execute his orders sooner. He affixed the seals, and we started off in a hack at ten o'clock at night. The coachman lost his way, and took us to the Rue St. Victor, where there was a house of detention. It was almost one o'clock when we reached La Grande Force; the prison for men was separate from that for women.

When it was proposed to leave Monsieur de Mouchy, at the former and take us to La Petite Force, I thought Madame de Mouchy, would die on the spot; and when it was necessary for her to separate from her husband, it was only by force that she could be torn from him and led away to a room where nineteen women were sleeping on hard beds of sacking. When she was brought to the door, the turnkeys, cross at being wakened from their sleep, hesitated about receiving her; but the clerk ordered them to do so. She wept the whole night long. She took it into her head that no arrangement had been made about my not being arrested, and that consequently I could not be allowed to remain. I told her that the commissioner had obtained an order from the Committee of General Security on the subject. He brought it to me at once. I was delighted at this piece of good fortune, which greatly comforted Madame de Mouchy, who told me that it helped her to bear her misfortunes. Our lodgings were changed, and we took possession of the new ones. We found in them the widow of the mayor of Cassel, whose husband had been guillotined eight days before. She was in despair. I saw her pass whole nights on her knees upon her bed, weeping and praying alternately. The apartment was at the top of the house in the quarter appropriated to the women of the town, who kept up, though in prison, a frightful noise from about five o'clock in the evening through the whole night. They came to see Madame de Mouchy, to assure her of their innocence, and to ask her to pay to them her garnish-money. In the morning she received a message from Monsieur de Mouchy, who proposed to her to go with him to the prison of the Luxembourg. She replied that 'since her separation from him she had never ceased to declare that she would give everything she had in the world to be able to be with him, even though she slept on a bed of straw.'

Some objections were made to this arrangement, but they were overcome. When I informed Madame la Maréchale that all was settled, she embraced me, and said, 'You could tell me of nothing which could make me so happy as this. Go at once and tell the ministering angel who enables me to rejoin

Monsieur de Mouchy, that I shall never forget the happiness he has procured for me.'

Commissioner Braut, who had been very severe to us at Mouchy, had become more lenient. It was he who had obtained our transfer to the Luxembourg. We went to La Grande Force for Monsieur de Mouchy. Never was there such an affecting reunion; even the turnkeys were touched by the sight, and so was Commissioner Braut.

We went almost joyfully to the Luxembourg. (Great God, how little one can tell what one may be glad to do.) Our conductor left us in the keeper's room. We remained there from five o'clock till nine. A terrible scene took place in that apartment; the famous Henriot, general of the Parisian army, came with his flute to look for a patriot who had been unjustly incarcerated at Caen, and afterward brought to Paris. He had taken a great deal of wine at a great dinner, where the guests made terrible jokes about the aristocrats, saying, with coarse laughter, 'Yes, we must have twenty thousand of those creatures' heads.' We had to wait until they were gone before we could know where we were to be lodged. The room assigned us was one formerly occupied by Brissot de Varville. The window was still walled up. Madame de Mouchy's, bed was set directly over the place where formerly stood the bed of her mother (Madame d'Arpajon had an apartment at the Luxembourg, being maid-of-honour to the Queen of Spain, Madame d'Orleans), who was lodging there at the time of Madame de Mouchy's birth. She frequently told us of having been born in the Luxembourg, of having been married there, and would add, 'and do you not think it strange that I should be imprisoned here?'

Although I did not really believe in the fate which actually threatened her, this speech made me shiver inwardly. The day after our arrival was spent entirely in getting ourselves settled to the best advantage in the small space allotted to us.

The day after, the commissioner Bétremieux came to take Monsieur and Madame de Mouchy to their house, so as to break the seals in their presence. They had the pleasure of meeting there Mesdames de Poix, and de Noailles. All passed off very well; nothing of a suspicious character was found. The *procès-verbal* was properly made out, and we had some hopes that they would be allowed to remain in their own house; but we returned that evening to the Luxembourg.

There were fifty-three persons there who were well known to them, as they came from the section about the fountain of Grenelle. An order was sent to transfer the women to the Anglaises; those of them who were married obtained permission to remain.

The keeper told me, as I had been told at La Petite Force, that he could not allow me to remain in the house without the permission of the committee. I told him that I had had that for La Force; he explained to me, very truly, that this could not be used at the Luxembourg. He advised me to send in a petition to be allowed to stay, and promised me to say nothing if I received no answer. I sent the petition, received no reply, and he said nothing about me. We had been ten days in that room when the commissioner Marinot (quite a well-known man) entered with one of his agents. I had just seen Monsieur Bétremieux, and had made him promise faithfully to come to see Madame de Mouchy. We were pressing around him to inquire of him whether there was any hope of being liberated. Marinot said to him, angrily, 'What are you doing here? You are up to some mischief! Get out!' I began to tremble with fright, fearing lest I had compromised Monsieur Bétremieux. This terrible man continued in the same tone: 'Why are there only three persons in this room? Five must be put here;' and he made a figure five with charcoal on the fireplace. Madame de Mouchy, said to him: 'Citizen, you do not think what you are saying; five persons cannot stay here.' 'Ah! why not?' 'I do not wish any one here but my husband.' 'I will give you some old men.' 'I will not have it so; give me, rather, another room.' 'I will see; there is another higher up.' He came back in half an hour, and said as he opened the door, 'I have found a very pretty room with a fine corridor, where you can take exercise.' I went up to see it, and also the 'fine corridor,' which was full of big rafters, against which one would strike one's head. This room had been used as an office by Monsieur de la Marlière. The place where the stove had been was newly plastered over, and the walls were all blackened. One cannot imagine a dirtier place; it took me all day and more to make it clean. A stove was put up in this room; but the fire could not be lighted in it when the wind was from the south.

A description of this room and its furniture will not be out of place. On one side of the doorway, to the right, was my bed of sacking, set lengthwise; I got into it at the foot. Monsieur de Mouchy's bed was next to mine, and Madame's was placed transversely. Under the roof was a table and some of our dresses; on the other side of the grated window we put the wood, two arm-chairs, two ordinary chairs, another little table on which were other articles of wearing apparel. There were some plank shelves to hold our dishes; and one corner in the corridor was reserved, to be used as a wardrobe. My bed was a pantry during the day, a seat in the evening; and Monsieur de Mouchy's bed was used in the same manner. We spent five months in that terrible place, where the most needy creature on the estates of Monsieur and Madame la Maréchale would not have been willing to live. Their virtues sustained them in a wonderful degree; they were an example and comfort to all who saw them. Their sweetness and goodness were unfailing.

I have often seen persons come to the house in despair, and utterly overwhelmed at finding themselves in such a place. Messieurs de Nicolaï and de Laborde were so overcome that they could not speak. My venerable friends comforted them, cheered them, and induced them to come to them for encouragement and strength. When the administrators arrived, with their caps pulled down over their eyes, to ask, 'Have you no petitions to send in?' 'No, citizen; only if you could have my daughter, who is at Chantilly, transferred to this place, I should be extremely glad.' One of them said, 'Yes; that ought to be done on account of their age.' However, no steps were taken in that direction till the arrival of Danton, Lacroix, and others.

On the 4th of December, 1793, Commissioner Bétremieux came to take Monsieur and Madame de Mouchy to Mouchy, to be present at the opening of the seals; they remained there three days, and breathed a little fresh air. During this time they tried, without success, to be allowed to visit their house in the company of keepers; nor could they obtain leave to see their daughter at Chantilly as they were on their way back to Paris. The commissioner finally took them to their own house, where they spent the day with their daughters-in-law. They were compelled to return to the Luxembourg in the evening. This parting was even more trying than the former ones; the few servants who had remained about the house hid their faces and wept.

We returned to the same way of living. Our days were passed in the following manner: Monsieur de Mouchy rose first, at an early hour, lighted his candle, said his prayers, and took a little coffee; then Madame de Mouchy rose and took her breakfast. As soon as she was dressed I went to wait upon Madame d'Hautefort, with whom they used to live; and then I returned and made my toilet. After this, they went out of the room so as to give me time to put it in order. At this hour they always went to see Madame la Duchesse d'Orleans, and they always came away filled with admiration for her angelic conduct. They never exhausted their praises of her,—an evidence of their own goodness. They returned to their own apartment about half-past twelve o'clock; at one, dinner was sent them from their own house. They never partook of this meal without speaking of Madame de Duras, longing for her, and grieving that they could not share it with her, knowing she had such miserable fare. Then some visitors would come in; after that Monsieur and Madame de Mouchy would go out to dine with a neighbour, and after their return would play piquet together. Monsieur de Mouchy then walked about the house. About five o'clock company assembled. The guests were sometimes too numerous for the size of our apartment, and also for my peace of mind, as I knew there were many spies about us. The person who was my greatest source of anxiety was the Prince of Hesse, who lodged near us, and invariably walked up and down continually in front of our door whenever we had several of our friends together. He was even seen with his ear against the door, trying to hear what we were saying. He informed against one of the keepers, who proved the charge to be false, and had him transferred to another prison, to my great delight. At eight o'clock every one left, and we had supper. Whenever we received any newspapers, they usually arrived at this hour. Toward the last I tried to find out in advance whether the names of the victims contained in them were of the persons whom Monsieur and Madame de Mouchy most dreaded to see in the list of the condemned; if so, I suppressed them until the next day. At ten o'clock we were all in bed.

A great change took place in Monsieur and Madame de Mouchy. He was naturally extremely vivacious and she very quiet; now he became calm and she exceedingly restless, especially so when on certain days she did not receive the usual communications which her daughter took such trouble to send, and when all sorts of unreliable news was brought by persons entering the prison. The nobles, particularly, were always sanguine. I have seen them make out plans of campaigns which would bring Cobourg to Paris, and even to the very doors of their prison, to conduct them in triumph to their own homes. These unfortunate persons lulled themselves with the false hopes lying so far in the distance and never perceived the precipices that were yawning beneath their feet.

During the period when we were allowed to go to the courtyard and speak to our friends through a grated window, each one would return and say, 'I have seen my wife (or my daughter, or my servant), who could not explain herself fully, but assured me by a pressure of the hand that all was going well.' If a person of any distinction was seen in the garden making the least possible signal of any kind it was sufficient to arouse hope. I certainly did not share the hopefulness enjoyed by most of the prisoners; indeed, it frightened me. I undertook at times to convince them that they were too sanguine; but I afterward reproached myself for taking the liberty to do so, for delusion was a necessity to them. Some persons deluded themselves so completely that they even found that there were some reasons why their friends and acquaintances should be condemned, but were confident that they should be exempt. Monsieur and Madame de Mouchy were not of this sort; on the contrary, they considered their situation a very critical one. One thing was done which alarmed us all; popular commissions were sent out by the Committee of General Security, containing questions to be answered by the prisoners. These questions were extremely captious. I think I can remember them exactly, and also Monsieur de Mouchy's answers.

By Order of the Committee of General Security,

QUESTIONS.	ANSWERS.
Your name?	Noailles Mouchy.
Your age?	In my seventy-ninth year.
Where did you live before and after the Revolution began, and since then?	In Paris, on the Rue de l'Université and since the 9th of September at Mouchy with my wife and my daughter.
Are you a married man? If so, how long since you were married?	I have been married fifty-two years to Anne Claude Louise d'Arpajon.
The number of your children, their age, and their whereabouts?	Three children: one daughter forty-nine years old, married to the former Duc de Duras, and now a prisoner at Chantilly; Phillippe de Poix, forty years, who left France to save his life, as a price was set on his head; Louis Noailles, aged thirty-seven, left France with all the pass-ports required at the time, and is now in North America.
Your profession before and since the Revolution?	I have been a soldier from my youth; and I have risen to the rank of Marshal of France.
Value of your property before and since the Revolution?	My income before the Revolution was more than a hundred thousand livres; for two years one of my estates in Languedoc has been under sequestration under pretext that I had emigrated (though this was proved not to be so), by order of the Committee of General Security. The subsidies and the forced loan, under which I have just been obliged to relinquish a considerable sum, render it impossible for me to furnish any correct valuation.
With whom have you associated before and	With my relatives both before and since.

since the Revolution?

Have you not signed resolutions derogatory to liberty?	I have never signed any resolutions.
What have you done for the Revolution?	All that was required of me.

Madame de Mouchy added:—

'Having been united to my husband for fifty-two years I have entertained no opinions differing from his.'

[Then followed their signatures.]

We had great difficulty in persuading Monsieur de Mouchy to agree to answer the aforesaid questions; at first he positively refused, declaring that he would never do anything so revolting. I consulted different members of his family and some of his companions in misfortune, who said that it was impossible for him to escape answering the questions, and that the answers given, and which I have just written down, were quite sufficient. There were always, they said, some etceteras. Certain persons of whom I have spoken, who were always too sanguine, thought that the interrogatories would hasten the acts of liberation; but, on the contrary, we were not left long in peace, and the harsh treatment increased. Then the conspiracy entered into by Vincent Savart and Grandmont (which I believe was the only real one) broke out. We were then forbidden to walk in the courtyard or to receive newspapers; and we were extremely restricted in every respect. After a while we were again allowed to have the newspapers, but never again to walk except in the galleries, where it was impossible to take a step without running into one another. So many persons were brought in that every place was full, although many were sent off to the tribunal every day.

Danton, Lacroix, Camille Desmoulins, etc. arrived. There was a knocking at our door at six o'clock, and we were told to prepare to move our quarters. The turnkey said to me 'Hurry! some fine people are coming and we need this room as a place of close confinement.' I asked him where the room was which was to be given us; he did not know, but the jailer who followed conducted me to it. It was, Monsieur and Madame de Mouchy thought, sufficiently large to accommodate their daughter, if she could be brought to the Luxembourg. There was a fireplace in it which gave me infinite satisfaction whenever I saw Monsieur de Mouchy warming himself in front of it; for he had been freezing for five months, as we had only one little stove, which gave me the headache whenever the fire was lighted in it.

On the 5th of April, 1794, about a fortnight after we had been established in our new lodgings, a convoy arrived from Chantilly. Monsieur Randon de la Tour, who was of the party, came very early in the morning to tell our distinguished old couple that Madame de Duras was in Paris, and had positively received orders to come to the Luxembourg during the day. They were perfectly delighted. But the whole day passed and she did not come; and we learned that she was at the Plessis. We hoped that she was there only temporarily; as she still did not come we sent the most urgent petitions to the administrators for her transfer. Hopes were held out to us, but Providence had decreed otherwise; and if our prayers had been answered, she would not now be living. After a while however we began to hope again. One day a man named Vernet said to me in a mysterious tone, 'There is some one of your acquaintance below whom the citizen Mouchy, will be glad to see.' I said, 'Surely it must be the Citizeness Duras.' (He knew that her father had asked to have her sent here as he had himself carried two messages to the Committee of General Security.) Vernet replied, 'I cannot say; there are several persons.' I ran to repeat the conversation to Monsieur and Madame de Mouchy, who did not doubt it was their daughter with other ladies whose husbands were in the Luxembourg and who had petitioned to be allowed to join them. We arranged the room so as to be able to put a bed in for her; and to our astonishment, after waiting a whole hour, Madame la Maréchale de Noailles, Madame la Duchesse d'Ayen, and Madame la Vicomtesse de Noailles entered. Monsieur de Mouchy was entirely upset by this. He had a very bad cold, and his fever rose immediately. He greatly dreaded the imprudence of his sister-in-law, who was very light-headed. He said that nothing could be more disagreeable to him than to have her so near him. These ladies told how, after having been tossed about from prison to prison, they had with much difficulty obtained permission to be sent to the Luxembourg that they might be near him. They were lodged above us in an *entresol*. The apartment was soon prepared. The furniture was very scanty, and I undertook to arrange it; I never saw worse beds. These ladies, like most of those who were condemned in advance, entered the prison feeling quite sure of being soon restored to liberty. As usual, only fifty francs had been left to each of them by the turnkeys; they were advised to provide themselves with a little more cash. Madame la Maréchale had twelve hundred francs and the Vicomtesse, her granddaughter, had two hundred francs. They were told that this would be enough for their expenses for a month. This money did not last them very long as it was all taken a short time after in the well remembered general search. The following is a detailed account of the manner in which our search was conducted. In the morning, as I opened the shutters of my room, I saw an armed guard in the courtyard,—an unusual circumstance. I went out into the corridor to get some wood which was piled up there, and found four musketeers at our doorway with the jailer, who said, 'Go back into your room, Citizeness.' I said, 'I am not going out; I am going to get some wood.' 'Go back, I tell you.' I obeyed trembling and fearing that something was about to happen to Monsieur and Madame la Maréchale. I went up to Madame la Maréchale's bed and said to her as quietly as possible, 'I don't know what is going on, but there are guards in the court and in the corridor, and the jailer would not allow me to get any wood.' She answered, 'I thought I heard them. My God! what can it be?' I went back to the window and saw that there were musketeers also on the pavilion opposite, which somewhat reassured me. I concluded that it was a general arrangement for the whole house. Two sentinels had been posted at our door, and I tried to have some talk with them. One good-natured fellow to whom I furtively gave a glass of wine said to me in a low voice: 'We do not know why we are here. Orders were sent to the section of the Observatory for us to rise at three o'clock this morning; we were led here, and ordered not to speak to any one nor to allow any one at all to come out of the apartments.' We did not learn very much from that interview. I made ten attempts to go up to see Mesdames de Noailles, but was always prevented. Nothing was allowed to enter the house; dinner was not brought in till five o'clock in the evening. We questioned the turnkeys, but they said that they knew nothing. We were obliged to go to bed without finding out anything about what was going on. The sentinels remained at our doors all night, or rather for four days, as we were among the last who were searched; and we had no communication with our neighbours till the second day, when one of them knocked gently at an unused door which opened into our apartment and told us that a very strict search was going on, that money, scissors, knives, etc. were being taken. We made the disclosure to Monsieur and Madame de Boisgelin in the same way. A man who waited upon them had gone out the day before to get some water and had not returned.

At last I obtained permission to go to see Mesdames de Noailles; the distinguished Vicomtesse had made the beds, washed the dishes, and in spite of all was in fine spirits. She joked about her labours, which were quite extensive, and the more so since the deafness of the three ladies caused them frequently to misunderstand one another. At night she tied one end of a string to her arm and the other to her grandmother's bed so that the latter might waken her if she needed her during the night. She dressed her, attended to an abscess she had, and also to one of her mother's. She had scarcely time to breathe, and her zeal stood her instead of natural strength. I had, as I have said, obtained permission to go and wait upon her. I had plenty to do, for I rendered the same services to Monsieur and Madame de Boisgelin.

Our turn to be searched came at last on the fourth day, at eleven o'clock in the morning. The sentinels had been withdrawn the day before, at ten o'clock at night. Monsieur de Baquencourt, who lodged in our quarter, took advantage of the first opportunity to come and tell us that the search was terrible, that a prisoner had assured him that he had been entirely stripped, that he had at first concealed his *assignats*, but had afterward shown them as he preferred to give up everything rather than to get into trouble. The idea of being stripped and searched worried us very much; but there was no getting out of it.

All took place as he foretold; the municipal authorities and the guards made the search. When they came to the *assignats* I said, 'Citizens, are you not going to count them?' One of them answered scornfully, 'We need not count them in order to conquer the enemies of the Republic.' 'I am sure of that,' I replied; 'for they could not be conquered with paper.' Madame de Mouchy, made a sign to me to be silent. Eight or ten days after, the committee ordered the account of each prisoner to be made out over again. This was done in the keeper's apartment. Then we went back to the same old life. We tried to get accustomed to doing without scissors and knives, but it was very inconvenient; and what was still more disagreeable, the turnkeys, who formerly could receive money for small services rendered, were forbidden to do so any longer, and this made them very cross. The establishment of a public table was also spoken of, which greatly distressed Madame de Mouchy. Soon after this a commission was appointed to examine the prisoners; a good many of them were anxious for it. The day it was announced loud cries of 'Vive la Republique!' were heard in the galleries. It did not take place, however, till two months afterward. One day about that time I was sitting at work when some one called for me. I found at the door the jailer (no longer the good Benoît) with two turnkeys, who asked me:

'What are you doing here?'

'I have been here for six months with the Citizen Mouchy and his wife.'

'Very well; but what are you doing here?'

'I do whatever I can for them.'

'Where is your entry in the jail-book?'

'I have none; I came here voluntarily.'

'You were not arrested, then?'

'No.'

'Are they their confidential friend?'

'Yes.'

'What is your name?'

I gave my signature. I asked him why he asked me all these questions. 'You are not going to send me away?'

'Oh, no! Benoît's papers are not properly drawn up, and I am taking a census of all who are in the house.'

Madame de Mouchy was very much agitated during this examination. She was reassured when she learned that it was only a census; but I was not. I endeavoured not to show to her the anxiety I felt and which was only too well founded.

One morning, about a month after this, the same jailer came into Madame la Maréchale's room and said to her: 'I have come to inform you that you must send away your confidential attendant within twenty-four hours; I have just received the order.' She replied, 'Citizen, I cannot do without her; I am very infirm, and so is my husband.' I asked him if I could stay if I became a prisoner. 'I do not know.' I begged him to send us the first prison-director who came to the place. He agreed to do so. I sent for Vernet, that he might speak for me. Madame de Mouchy was so good as to implore him so earnestly to do me this service that I could not help shedding tears; she offered to give him all the jewels and *assignats* she had left. He would not accept anything; but promised to do all we asked, and did nothing. I gave him a petition I had written to the Committee of Police, in which I requested most earnestly to be enrolled as a prisoner. I represented to them the infirm condition of Monsieur and Madame de Mouchy, how impossible it was for them to be left alone, how long I had been with them, and added that I thought it a Republican virtue to assist suffering humanity. At the same time I asked the jailer to allow me to wait for an answer; and I begged Vernet to bring the administrator to us, which he did on the following day.

It was Vitrich, who has since died, with his friend Robespierre. He said to me, 'We have read your petition. You are very good to wait upon these old people; but I have nothing to do with that. The order is from the Committee of General Security, and you must go. You have only to make a similar petition to them, and surely you will receive their permission to return.' I begged him with tears, for I was desperate, for permission to remain till the next day; and he granted it.

I cannot express the horrors of our situation after this cruel sentence. Dear, venerable old couple, how much they suffered! This separation seemed only to presage one more terrible still. We wept all night long. I was almost determined to remain, no matter what happened to me. For three whole days my daughter never left the door in her anxiety to hear from the turnkeys what I had concluded to do. She was terribly frightened about me. A prisoner, whom I did not know, influenced me to a decision; he stopped me and said, 'Citizeness, I have learned that you are hesitating about leaving here; I think I ought to tell you that you are doing wrong. This evening you will be entered in the jail-book, and perhaps sent to-morrow to another prison; the greater attachment you manifest for Madame de Mouchy the more you will be suspected. Believe me, you had better submit. A more favourable moment will surely come, and you can then rejoin her; above all conceal your tears, for you are watched.' I thanked him, and informed Monsieur and Madame de Mouchy of his advice. They then urged me to go. We consulted together as to what I was to do in order to be allowed to return. Hoping to certainly do so, I left all my belongings. Messieurs d'Hénin and de Boisgelin assured me that the separation would not be long, and that as soon as I should see the committee I could ask that Madame de Duras might be sent to join her parents; and they would surely grant my request.

When the fatal moment arrived I felt that it would be utterly impossible for me to say to Monsieur and Madame de Mouchy, 'I am going to leave you now;' so I said that I was going to see some of the prisoners to ask for messages from them. They all sympathized with my sorrow. Madame la Vicomtesse de Noailles, the younger, threw her arms around me, and burst into tears. I tore myself from her, and hid behind a door, to try and recover myself. As I passed along the galleries all the prisoners congratulated me; for my part I wished they were all in my place. When I reached the door I thought I should faint; I wanted to go in to see the keeper, but the turnkey who had the key prevented me. 'Take care!' said he to me, 'there is a clerk in his office who is vexed with you; go on.' I cannot express all the different feelings which assailed me on getting into the street; my despair at leaving Monsieur and Madame de Mouchy, my reunion with my daughter, the open air which I had not breathed for seven months,—all bewildered me. One thing is certain, I could not tell what streets I passed through on my way to the Hôtel Mouchy. Instead of seeming delighted to see my daughter, I replied to all she said only with tears.

The first thing I did was to beg Monsieur Noël to send my petition to the committee as soon as possible, which he did. He received no reply. It was impossible to gain an interview. I did not know to whom to apply. Madame de Poix, was at the Hôtel Mouchy, under guard. She had been imprisoned only twenty-four hours on account of her weakness. She asked me many questions concerning her distinguished parents, wept much with me, and still hoped that I might be able to return to them. I had an opportunity to see the deputies from my district, who had just saved my brother from the guillotine. I thought they would be willing to render me a service also. I implored them in vain, however, and received from them only mockery of my attachment, and the most positive refusal. At last, repulsed in every direction, nothing was left but to have myself arrested. This was my plan; I thought of it unceasingly. The only thing that prevented me was the almost complete certainty of being sent to some other prison than the Luxembourg. The tidings I received from day to day were more and more distressing. Monsieur de Mouchy wrote me: 'Come back to us; Madame de Mouchy, has been so grieved at your absence that her abscess has dried up,—a thing which never happened before.' Another time he said, 'We cannot get accustomed to your absence, nor to doing without you. The two or three persons who wait upon us, no matter how willing they may be, cannot accomplish in the whole day what our dear Latour used to do in two hours, and without difficulty.'

All this went to my heart. I wrote to them every day, and gave them more hope of my returning to them than I entertained myself. I went frequently to carry them provisions, as well as to learn how they were from the turnkeys, who were on good terms with me. I also went into the garden, where I had the sad consolation of seeing them at the window. The prisoners knew me so well that as soon as they saw me they would hasten to tell my friends. Their sad and downcast faces broke my heart. I dared not make the least sign to them as I was constantly watched. The last day that I went there with my daughter a man followed us persistently, and drove us away. My daughter was sure then that we were going to be arrested. It was the last time that I ever saw Madame de Mouchy. Two days after, Monsieur de Mouchy, sent me word that 'she had had a severe attack of indigestion, accompanied by violent vomiting, all through the night; that they needed me more than ever.' He told me to send him a bottle of mineral water for her to take as a purgative. The day she took it, Monsieur le Maréchal wrote me at four o'clock in the afternoon that the purgative had not agreed with her at all, that Madame la Maréchale could not retain any nourishment, and requested me to send her an injection immediately. I was extremely anxious. It was too late for me to be able to speak to any one, as all the doors were closed at five o'clock. I determined to go to see the turnkey early the next morning, and find out whether I might be allowed to wait upon her; but it was then too late. Everything was useless; the end of all their troubles was approaching.

Just as I was getting into my bed there was a loud knocking at my door. I trembled as I opened it. I was surprised to see Monsieur Noël, who looked frightened, and said, 'A messenger was sent to the Luxembourg this evening to inquire whether Monsieur and Madame de Mouchy were there, and I cannot imagine what it means.' I cried, 'It is well known that they are in that house, and such inquiries are superfluous,—unless,' I added, seeing that his agitation was increasing, 'Madame la Maréchale, being ill, has asked for me again, and some prison-director has been to inquire into her condition.' 'I hope it may be so, I will learn to-morrow morning early what it is all about, and will come and tell you.' We spent the night in the greatest excitement, and I rose very early. I went to Monsieur Noël's house at seven o'clock, but he had already gone out. He came to my house crying, or rather screaming, 'It is true,' said he; 'all is over! They are at the Conciergerie.' Nothing else that I have ever suffered in my life can be compared to what I felt at that moment. However, I did not altogether lose my self-control; enough was left me to see that poor Monsieur Noël was entirely beside himself. He beat his head so violently against the wall that I really feared he would crush it. After the first moments of his despair had passed, he said, 'I will go out again; I will go to the Conciergerie; I must see them!' 'And I will go too,' I cried. 'No, no,' he answered. 'Is Madame de Duras there?' 'I have not been able to learn.'

He returned about nine o'clock in the morning. 'Well,' said I, 'have you heard anything? Is there no hope?' 'No, no,' was all his answer. 'And Madame de Duras?' 'She is not there.' He asked me to go and tell the sad news to Madame de Poix. I should have been glad to be spared this, for I scarcely had the strength to do it; but he went out again, and I was obliged to go also. She was in absolute despair. Monsieur Noël advised me to go away from the house, lest I should be sent for as a witness. I would not do so. I did not know where to go; I preferred, I said, to die with them rather than after them. At last I was persuaded to go to the house of one of my friends.

Before going, however, I charged them to take some dinner to the Conciergerie. It was possible that these precious victims might remain there several days. They sent it back with their thanks, but untouched.

At five o'clock in the evening I left my friend's house, being no longer able to resist the desire to hear what was going on; I met my daughter coming to see me. Her agitated countenance confirmed my fears. I met Monsieur Noël; he said not a word to me as he passed me, nor I to him. We did not even dare to look at each other. I went the next day again to see Madame de Poix, whose whole appearance was utterly changed. She had lost not only her distinguished parents but Madame de Biron, her intimate friend from childhood. She asked me kindly what I was going to do. 'Nothing,' I answered, 'but await my fate here.' I thought that, not having been able to share that of Monsieur and Madame de Mouchy, I might be allowed to follow that of Madame de Duras, believing that none of us would escape death. Madame de Noailles wrote me three or four days after our loss a note which I am inconsolable at having burned, but I was compelled to do so. It contained such a touching description of how Monsieur and Madame de Mouchy remembered me in their last moments, and expressions of Madame de Mouchy's sympathy in my sorrow in spite of all her own suffering, that it caused me, for the first time, to give way to tears. Until then I had been like a stone.

Within ten days after the death of my honoured master and mistress, I was called upon to mourn for all those of their acquaintance at the Luxembourg who had shown me much kindness, among them Mesdames d'Hautefort, Madame de Noailles, and others. Twenty days later we sent some linen to Madame de Duras, which was not received; this frightened us on her account, for we feared she was no longer there. And finally I became terrified on my own account. I had the greatest possible horror of death. I feared I never should have sufficient resignation to endure the last twenty-four hours; but I hoped that my courage would not fail me in my last moments if I could be with those from whom I could receive consolation. The preparations for execution made me cold with fright. I felt that the courage which would have enabled me to bear anything in company with Monsieur and Madame de Mouchy, had abandoned me. On the other hand it was strange that I should have such a terror of death, being otherwise perfectly indifferent concerning my fate. My relatives and friends pitied me, not only on account of the loss I had just sustained, but on account of my financial position, knowing that I had no means at all. I answered that this did not concern me in the least. My mind continually reverted to what Monsieur de Mouchy had said to me one day: he thanked me for a small service I had rendered him, and added, 'God will reward you, my dear child, for all the trouble you have taken for me. I am sure you will never want for anything.'

I was obliged, in spite of all my indifference to fate, to ask to have back again the furniture of my room, for which I had to pay four hundred francs, with a guarantee from Monsieur Noël. We left that house after having drunk the cup of sorrow to the dregs, having seen it all stripped of furniture and thrown into utter disorder. The commissioners received from our hands everything belonging to Monsieur de Mouchy and Madame la Maréchale, treating the things in the most insulting and indecent manner.

Robespierre was beheaded. Madame de Duras was liberated the 16th of October, 1794. But, oh, how changed she was! It was dreadful to see her. She seemed, as she said herself, like one risen from the dead. In spite of her trials it was evident that her courage had not failed. Her first thought, and also that of Madame de Poix, on being once more in the enjoyment of liberty, was to see that I had means of support, and to find out all ways of rendering me assistance.

12. The *féodiste* [steward] was named Carbonnier. He as well as his wife gave proof of the sincerest attachment and fidelity to Monsieur and Madame de Mouchy. He was imprisoned for a whole year in the Anglaises and the Grande Force.

EVENTS OF THE 21st OF JULY, 1794.

MONSIEUR GRELET'S ACCOUNT.

It was the 21st of July, 1794 (2d Thermidor, year II.); I was on my way to the Luxembourg at half past seven o'clock in the evening, to carry to Madame de Noailles a bundle containing some wearing apparel. When I reached the lower end of the Rue de Tournon, I saw in front of the door of that prison a great mob of men and women, which made me feel very anxious. I deposited my bundle in a shop on that street where a young woman stayed who was the friend of Madame la Duchesse d'Ayen's waiting-woman, and went on toward the prison.

When I came among the crowd I had no difficulty in discovering what was going on, particularly when I saw a great open wagon with benches fastened along the sides. I knew at once that it was there to receive the prisoners who were to be transferred to the Conciergerie to be beheaded the next day; this thought made me shiver. I had a presentiment that the ladies in whom I was interested would be among the victims. I was anxious to see the prisoners taken away, and approached the door as nearly as I possibly could. A turnkey came out, and perceiving me said, 'Go away; they are coming.'

I did not go away. I thought it would be the last time I should ever see those ladies, and this sad thought rooted me to the spot. The turnkey went in again. A little while after the door opened and the prisoners appeared, preceded by two gendarmes. Madame la Vicomtesse de Noailles was the first of the ladies to come out. She passed very near me, took my hand and pressed it affectionately. The gendarme who walked beside her assisted her to get into the wagon. Madame d'Ayen and Madame la Maréchale got in immediately after her. One of the gendarmes had seen Madame de Noailles give me her hand. Then five or six other ladies got in and as many men as it would hold. I moved away and tried to conceal myself in the crowd. Madame de Noailles still saw me, however, for the wagon had not yet started. As it would not hold all the prisoners, about fifteen of them followed on foot, escorted by gendarmes. While all the preparations for this transfer were being made, Madame de Noailles, who again recognized me, clasped her hands, made me a sign to pray and that she was praying. A moment afterward she lifted her head, and pointing with one finger to heaven she gave me her blessing. The crowd wondered to whom her gestures were addressed; and I gazed as others did, trying to act just as though they were not addressed to me. Madame de Noailles apprised her mother that I was near the wagon. Madame d'Ayen bowed and kissed her hand to me several times. I could not take any notice of this; such gestures alone would have been more than sufficient to compromise me.

At last, after half an hour spent in preparation, the wagon started and went down the Rue de Condé. I followed it as far as the Conciergerie. About midway this street, in a part of it which is very narrow, I could almost touch at the same time both the houses at the side and the wagon. Madame de Noailles, who never lost sight of me, gave me her blessing three times,— one for each of her children. I continued to follow the wagon as I would have followed the funeral procession of persons whose death was to plunge so many families into such terrible grief.

As I was crossing the Pont Neuf, the wagon being not far off and just turning round the Quai des Lunettes, a gendarme called out behind me, 'I arrest you; I know you.' I did not give him a chance to arrest me but ran along the Quai des Lunettes. The gendarme followed me; I ran down the Rue de Harlay, which crosses the Island of the Palace. The gendarme was far behind me crying, 'Stop him!' It was eight o'clock,—just the hour when the workmen were leaving their shops. They thought I was a prisoner escaping; several tried to stop me, but I kept them off with my cane. On reaching the Quai des Orfèvres I fell, and was seized by two workmen; the gendarme over-took me, and I made no further effort to escape. A man came up who said he was a justice of the peace, and inquired of the gendarme why he had arrested me. The gendarme replied that I was intriguing with the prisoners. I thought it useless to attempt to defend myself. As the gendarme was taking me to the prefecture of police, I saw some distance off Madame de Noailles and the other prisoners going into the prison of the Conciergerie.

I was put into a dungeon where there was a small window, which admitted only a few rays of light. I took advantage of this to destroy some papers which would have been sufficient to compromise me. Fortunately I preserved my *carte de sûreté*, which I had only had a few days. I had just torn up and destroyed the papers, part of which I swallowed, when the door opened and showed me a jailer, who ordered me in menacing tones to follow him. After having led me through some dark corridors he shut me in a very small dungeon, secured by an iron door, through which no light could penetrate. This dungeon was circular in form and extremely small. There was a stone bench against the wall. As I entered I had seen by the light of the lamp carried by the jailer something on the floor which sparkled. When the dungeon door was closed on me I was in total darkness. I felt around to find out what had occasioned the flashes of light to which I have referred. I found that they proceeded from some bits of glass which were on the edge of a very small opening made in the wall. I seated myself on the stone bench and began to reflect on my situation, on that of Mesdames de Noailles, whom I had just seen for the last time, and on that of their poor children, who were waiting for me before going to their evening meal. Then I realized all the horrors of my situation. And when I thought of all that was to take place the next day, I fell on my knees and prayed to God with all the fervour of which I was capable. I implored him to accept the sacrifice of my life in expiation of my sins; for I expected to perish the next day. But what would become of those three children? What terrible grief it would be to their mother and grandmother to see me condemned with them! 'My God,' I prayed, 'have mercy on the children, have mercy on their mothers, and have mercy on me!'

I was utterly overcome by these sad reflections when the door opened with a loud noise. I rose suddenly, not knowing what might be going to happen. There was the jailer again, with his lantern, and an officer of the gendarmerie was with him. 'Have you your *carte*?' said the latter to me. I answered that I had. 'Give it to me.' 'Will you allow me,' said I, as I handed it to him, 'to tell you what took place, and why I am here?' 'Yes, you may tell me.' I related in a few words how I had happened by chance to be in front of the prison of the Luxembourg when the prisoners who were to be taken to the Conciergerie came out; that one of them, as she passed very near me, recognized me and pressed my hand, but that she did not speak a single word to me, nor did I to her; and that this was all that passed. After listening to me attentively he went away, and took my *carte* with him; but he had me put into more comfortable quarters.

My anxiety increased when I saw that he had carried off my *carte*, for it contained my address; and I was sure that they would go immediately to the Hôtel Noailles-Mouchy, on the Rue de l'Université, where my pupils Alfred and Alexis were. 'They will search all over the Hôtel,' said I to myself. 'They will find the whole of my correspondence with Madame de Noailles during her imprisonment; and as there are many things in those letters which are covertly expressed, they will be sure to find in them all sorts of intrigues relative to the conspiracy of the Luxembourg, about which the Republicans and Revolutionary judges are already making so much noise.' It is true that I had taken great care to conceal this correspondence. I had confided to Alexis the secret of the place where I had locked it up, and had charged him to put it out of sight if he should see the commissioners or any strangers coming to the Hôtel. We occupied the apartment of their father, the Vicomte de Noailles, the windows of which looked out into the street, in front of the main entrance. Though this thought somewhat reassured me, my anxiety continued, and the more so as the officer did not return, and it was now very late. I no longer doubted that he had been to pay a visit to the Hôtel Mouchy. 'But even if he should find nothing,' said I to myself, 'can any one ever escape who has once fallen into their hands?'

Such was the state of my anxiety when the officer returned and said these few words which I shall never forget. 'Here is your *carte*. Now go; and another time do not come so near.' I did not wait for him to say anything more. I took my *carte*, my cane, and the other things which had not been left with me were returned, and I was free!

I experienced a feeling of delight at being liberated contrary to my expectation; but this sweet content was only momentary. I thought of Mesdames de Noailles, whom I had left as it were in the ante-chamber of death. I could think of nothing else; at least they would not suffer the pain of seeing me share their fate on the morrow, and of thinking that their children were left without any one to care for them. 'Religion will come to their aid,' I thought; 'but what a struggle they will have to go through.' I gave thanks to God, and implored him to come to their help in this moment so full of horror to human creatures; and still praying as I went, I reached the Hôtel Mouchy. It was eleven o'clock. The children had not gone to bed; they were waiting for me. They asked me a great many questions, and told me that they had been very much frightened when I did not return. I told them that I had had a great many things to attend to which had caused me most unwillingly to delay; that I had been very much occupied; that I could not tell them then all that had happened to me because it was too late, but that I would tell them all about it the next day. We then said our prayers together and went to bed. 'At least,' said I to myself, 'they shall pass this night in peace; the next will be cruel and bitter enough.'

The next day (the 22d of July), while the children were still asleep, I went very early to the Rue des Sts. Pères, to see Père Brun, to tell him that the Mesdames de Noailles were at the Conciergerie to be tried, and would very probably be condemned to death that very day, and to beg him to keep the promise he had made me, which was to try to meet them as they passed from the prison to the extreme end of the Faubourg St. Antoine, as this was the only consolation they could now have in this world. He promised me he would not fail to be there. Whenever he could, this good priest exercised this act of charity toward the victims. He would accompany them, praying as he went, to the foot of the scaffold, and there give them the last absolution. After the deed was done he would return to his house, still praying, but with an aching heart.

Father Brun was a father of the Oratory. We had lived together at Juilly, where we had charge of the Pensioners called *Minimes*, because they were the youngest and the smallest. He was for a short time the curate of the parish of Juilly. Madame la Vicomtesse de Noailles, whose children, Alexis and Alfred, were in our hall, had corresponded with him for almost a year. She had great confidence in him, and he deserved it on account of his piety and his tender care of her children.

I returned to the Hôtel Mouchy. It was almost six o'clock. I awakened the children, and told them that we were going to see their sister Euphémie at St. Mandé, which pleased them very much. They never suspected the terrible tidings I had to tell them till we came to the end of our walk.[13]

---

13. A copy of this account was sent, May 21, 1850, to Madame la Marquise de Vérac by Monsieur Gérin, Monsieur Grelet's testamentary executor, and was declared by him to agree in every respect with the original from the hand of Monsieur Grelet.

NARRATIVE OF AN EYE-WITNESS OF THE AFFAIR OF JULY 22, 1794.

(M. CARRICHON, Priest.)

Madame la Maréchale de Noailles, her daughter-in-law, the Duchesse d'Ayen, and her granddaughter, the Vicomtesse de Noailles, were detained in their Hôtel from the month of September, 1793, until April, 1794. I knew the first by sight, and was better acquainted with the other two, whom I was accustomed to visit once a week.

The Terror was increasing, with its attendant crimes, and the victims were becoming more numerous. One day when we were speaking of this, and were exhorting each other to prepare to be among their number, I said to them with a sort of presentiment, 'If you go to the guillotine, and God gives me the strength, I will accompany you.' They took me at my word, adding with eagerness, 'Do you promise it?' I hesitated a moment. 'Yes,' I replied, 'and that you may be certain to recognize me I will wear a dark blue coat and a red waistcoat.'

After that they often reminded me of my promise. In the month of April, the week after Easter, I believe, they were conducted to the Luxembourg. I often received news of them through Monsieur Grelet, who with such delicate faithfulness rendered many services to them and to their children.

My promise was frequently recalled. On the 26th or 27th, a Thursday or a Friday, he came and begged me to render to the Maréchal de Mouchy and his wife the service which I had promised to them.

I went to the Palace and succeeded in making my way into the courtyard; I then had them under my eyes, and quite near me, for more than a quarter of an hour. Monsieur and Madame de Mouchy, whom I had seen at their house only once, and whom I knew better than they knew me, could not recognize me. By inspiration, and with the aid of God, I did what I could for them. The Maréchal's conduct was singularly edifying; he prayed aloud with great fervour. The evening before, on leaving the Luxembourg, he had said to those who regarded him with interest: 'At seventeen I went up to the assault for my king; at seventy-eight I go to the scaffold for my God; my friends, I am not unhappy.'

I avoid details which would lead me on to endless length. That day I believed it to be useless to attempt anything; and, indeed, I did not feel myself able to go and accompany them to the guillotine. I was much disturbed by this on account of the special promise made to their relatives, whom their death plunged into affliction. They were incarcerated in the same prison, and had done much to console the Maréchal de Mouchy and his wife.

How much might I say of all the many departures which preceded or followed that of the 22d of July!—departures, peaceful or wretched, according to the dispositions of those who departed. Terribly sad they were, even when the known character and all external signs denoted Christian resignation and a Christian death, but exceedingly distressing when the contrary was the case, and when the condemned appeared, as it were, to pass from a hell in this world to that of the other world.

On the 22d of July, which was Tuesday, I was at my house between eight and ten o'clock in the morning. I was just on the point of going out when I heard a knock on my door; I opened it and saw the children of the house of Noailles and their tutor. The children had the gayety natural to their age,— gayety which was to be changed to sadness by the losses they were about to undergo, and the fear of experiencing still others. They were going to walk.

The tutor, sad and melancholy, was pale and troubled. 'Let us go into your chamber,' said he, 'and leave the children in your study.' We went into the chamber; he cast himself into a chair. 'It is all over, my friend; the ladies are before the Revolutionary tribunal. I have come to summon you to keep your word. I am to take the children to Vincennes, and there see little Euphémie. In the park I will prepare the poor children for their terrible loss.'

Prepared as I was myself for this dreadful blow, I was overwhelmed. The frightful situation of the mothers, of the children, of their worthy tutor, this gayety to be followed by such depth of sorrow, the little sister, Euphémie, then about four years old,—all this arose before my imagination.

I recovered myself; and after some inquiries, replies, and other sad details, I said, 'I will now change my dress. What an errand! Pray to God that he may give me the strength to execute it.'

We arose and went out into the study, where we found the children amusing themselves innocently, gay and contented as could be. The sight of them, the thought of their ignorance, and of what they were about to learn, the interview with their sister which would follow, and that which we had just gone through, made the contrast more striking, and afflicted the heart.

Left alone after their departure, I felt myself overwhelmed and wearied. 'My God,' I cried, 'have pity upon them and upon me!' I changed my clothes and went upon certain errands, carrying in my heart a crushing weight.

I went to the palace between one o'clock and two, and tried to enter; it was impossible. I got some news from one who was coming out of the Court. I still doubted the reality of what he told me. The illusion of hope was finally destroyed by what he went on to say, and I could no longer have any doubts.

I renewed my walk. It took me to the Faubourg St. Antoine, and with what thoughts, what inward agitation, what secret fear, all joined to a violent headache!

I consulted a person in whom I had confidence. She encouraged me in the name of God. I took a little coffee at her house, and felt my head improved. I returned to the palace with slow steps, pensive and irresolute, dreading to reach the fatal spot, and hoping that I might not find those who summoned me there.

I arrived before five o'clock. Nothing indicated the departure of the prisoners. I went sadly up the steps of the Sainte-Chapelle; I walked in and around the great hall, I sat down, I rose again, I spoke to no one. I concealed within me the sorrow which was preying upon me. From time to time I cast a sad glance toward the courtyard, to see if any preparations for the procession were being made.

My continual thought was, 'In two hours, in one hour, they will be no more.' I cannot express how this idea, which has afflicted me all my life in the too frequent and distressing occasions in which it has been recalled, afflicted me at that time. With so dreadful a cause of waiting, never did an hour appear to me at once so long and so short as that which I passed from five o'clock to six, by reason of the various thoughts which agitated me, and which rapidly drove my mind from the illusions of a vain hope to fears unhappily only too real.

Finally, by the noise which came to my ears, I judged that the prison doors were about to be opened. I went down and took a position near the gate, as for a fortnight it had no longer been possible to obtain entrance into the courtyard.

The first cart was filled and came toward where I stood. It contained eight ladies who seemed in a very edifying frame of mind; they were unknown to me. The ninth and last, to whom I was very near, was the Maréchale de Noailles. The absence of her daughter-in-law and granddaughter gave me one last faint ray of hope. But alas! they immediately entered the second cart. Madame de Noailles was dressed in white, which she had not ceased wearing since the death of her father-in-law and mother-in-law, the Maréchal de Mouchy and his wife. She appeared about twenty-four years old at the most. Madame d'Ayen, a lady of forty years, was in a striped *déshabillé* of blue and white. I saw them, though at a little distance. Six men also got into the fatal car and took their places near them. I remarked that the first two took their stand at a little distance from the others, showing them by this respectful attention that they desired to leave them more free. From this I drew good auguries.

Scarcely had they taken their places when the daughter exhibited toward the mother an eager and tender interest, which was remarked by all the bystanders. I heard them saying near me, 'Do you see how agitated that young lady is, and how she talks to the other one?'

I saw that they were looking for me. I seemed to hear all that they said. 'Mamma, he is not there.'

'Look again.'

'Nothing escapes me, I assure you, Mamma; he is not there.'

They forgot that I had sent word to them of the impossibility of getting into the courtyard.

The first cart stood near me at least a quarter of an hour. It came forward first. The second was about to pass, and I stood ready. It passed, and the ladies did not see me. I went back into the palace, made a long circuit, and placed myself in a conspicuous position at the entrance of the Pont au Change. Madame de Noailles looked around on every side, but passed by without seeing me. I followed them along the bridge, separated from the crowd, and yet quite near them. Madame de Noailles, though constantly looking for me, did not perceive me.

Distress was painted upon the face of Madame d'Ayen; her daughter redoubled her watchfulness but without success. I was tempted to give up. I had done what I could, I said to myself, and everywhere else the crowd would be still greater. It was of no use, and I was tired. I was about to go away, when the sky was covered over, thunder was heard in the distance, and I resolved to make another trial.

By roundabout ways I arrived before the carts did in the Rue St. Antoine beyond the Rue de Fourcy, almost opposite the too famous prison of La Force. Then a violent wind arose. The storm burst; flashes of lightning and peals of thunder succeeded each other rapidly. The rain began, and soon fell in torrents. I withdrew to the doorway of a shop which I still vividly remember, and which I never since then see without emotion. In an instant the street was cleared; there were no more people, save at the doors, in the shops, and at the windows. There was more order in the marching. The horsemen and musketeers advanced more quickly, and the carts also. They reached the little St. Antoine, and I was still undecided. The first cart passed before me. A rapid and almost involuntary movement brought me from the shop door and to the second cart; and there I was alone, quite near the ladies. Madame de Noailles, smiling, seemed to say to me, 'Here you are at last; ah, how comforted we are! We have sought for you eagerly. Mamma, here he is.' Madame d'Ayen revived. All my irresolution ceased; I felt myself inspired by the grace of God with extraordinary courage. Though wet through with perspiration and rain I took no thought of it, but continued to walk near them. Upon the steps of the College St. Louis I perceived a friend, full of respect and attachment for them, endeavouring to render them the same service as that which I was offering them.[14] His face and attitude showed all that he felt upon seeing them. I struck my hand upon his shoulder with inexpressible emotion, and cried to him as I passed by, 'Good evening, my friend.'

At this point there is an open place, and several streets enter into it. The storm was at its height, and the wind had grown more violent. The ladies in the first wagon were much disturbed by it, especially the Maréchale de Noailles; her large cap was thrown back, and showed her gray hair. They tottered upon their rough plank seats, their hands being tied behind their backs. Immediately a crowd of men, who were there in spite of the rain, recognized her, paid attention only to her, and by their insulting cries increased the tortures which she was supporting with patience. 'There she is,' they cried, 'the Maréchale who went in such style, driving in her fine carriage,—there she is in the cart, just like the others!'

The cries continued; the heavens grew darker and the rain more violent. We reached the street crossing just in front of the Faubourg St. Antoine. I went forward, looked around, and said to myself, this is the best place to afford them what they so much desire. The cart was going more slowly; I stopped and turned toward them. I made a sign to Madame de Noailles which she entirely understood: 'Mamma, Monsieur Carrichon is about to give us absolution.' Immediately they bent their heads with an air of repentance, contrition, tenderness, hope, and piety.

I raised my hand, and, though with covered head, pronounced the entire formula of absolution, and the words which follow it, very distinctly, and with the deepest earnestness. They joined in this more perfectly than ever. I can never forget the holy picture, worthy of the pencil of Raphael, of that moment when, for them, all was balm and consolation.

Immediately the storm relaxed and the rain diminished. It was as if they had come only to insure the success of what my friends and I had so ardently desired. I blessed God for it, and they did the same. Their appearance showed contentment, security, and cheerfulness.

As we advanced into the Faubourg the eager crowds fell back upon the two sides of the street. They insulted the first ladies, especially the Maréchale; nothing was said to the other two. Sometimes I preceded and sometimes I accompanied the wagons. After passing the Abbey de St. Antoine I met a young man whom I had formerly known; he was a priest whom I had some reason to suspect, and his presence annoyed me. I was afraid of being recognized, but happily I was not; he turned aside, and I did not see him again.

Finally, we arrived at the fatal spot; what went on within me cannot be described. What a moment! What a separation, what grief for the husbands, the children, the sisters, the relatives and friends who should survive them in this vale of tears! 'I see them,' I thought, 'still full of health; they would have been so useful to their families, and in a moment I shall see them no more. How heart-rending it is! But what a great comfort to us to see them so resigned!'

The scaffold appears; the carts come to a stop; the guards surround them; I shudder. A more numerous circle of spectators now is about us; most of them laugh, and are amused at this heart-breaking spectacle. Imagine how terrible a situation it was for me, to be in the midst of such a crowd with my mind agitated by thoughts so different.

While the executioner and his two attendants were assisting the ladies who were in the first cart to descend, Madame de Noailles's eyes wandered around in search of me. At last she saw me. And now there was a repetition of that first ravishing view I had of her. Her expressive eyes, so sweet, so animated, so heavenly, glanced first up to heaven and then down to earth, and finally were fixed so intently upon me that it might have caused me to be remarked if my neighbours had been more attentive. I pulled my hat down over my eyes, but not so as to prevent my seeing her. I seemed to hear her say, 'Our sacrifice is made. We leave our dear ones; but God in his mercy calls us. Our faith is firm. We shall not forget them when we are in his presence. We give you our thanks, and send our tenderest farewells to them. Jesus Christ, who died for us, is our strength. We die in his arms. Farewell! God grant we may all meet again in heaven. Farewell!'

It is impossible to give any idea of her saintly, earnest gestures; there was about her an eloquence so touching that those around me said, 'Ah, see that young woman! How resigned she is! See how she raises her eyes to heaven! See how she is praying! But what good will that do her?' Then on reflection: 'Oh, those wicked parsons!' Having said their last farewells they all descended from the wagon.

I was no longer conscious of anything, being at once heart-broken, grieved, and yet comforted. How I thanked God that I had not delayed giving them absolution till this moment! If I had waited till just as they were mounting the scaffold we could not have been so united in the presence of God to ask and receive this great blessing as we had been in the other place; and that also was the most undisturbed moment of the whole route.

I leave the spot where I had been standing. I pass round to the opposite side while the others are getting out of the wagon. I find myself in front of the wooden stairway by which they were to mount the scaffold, and against which a tall, rather fat old man with white hair and a kindly face was leaning. He looked like a farmer. Near him was a very resigned-looking woman whom I did not know; next came the Maréchale de Noailles, just opposite me, dressed in black taffeta. She had not yet laid aside mourning for the Maréchal. She was seated on a block of wood or stone which happened to be there, her large eyes fixed. I did not forget to pray for her as I had done for so many others, and especially for the Maréchal and Maréchale de Mouchy. All the others were ranged in two lines on the side facing the Faubourg St. Antoine.

I looked around for the ladies; I could only see the mother. Her attitude was that of devotion,—simple, noble, and resigned. Entirely occupied with the sacrifice she was about to offer to God through the merits of the Saviour, his divine son, her eyes were closed; she showed no anxiety, not even as much as when formerly she had had the privilege of approaching the sacred table. I shall never forget the impression she made upon me then. I often picture her to myself in that attitude. God grant that I may profit by it.

The Maréchale de Noailles was the third to mount the altar of sacrifice. It was necessary to cut away the upper part of the neck of her dress so as to expose her throat. I felt as if I could not stand and see it all; yet I wished to drink the cup to the dregs and keep my word, if only God would grant me strength to keep my senses in the face of such a terrible sight.

Six ladies passed on after her. Madame d'Ayen was the tenth. She seemed to me to look pleased that she was to die before her daughter did, and the daughter glad to die after her mother. When she mounted the scaffold the chief executioner pulled off her bonnet. As it was fastened on by a pin which he did not take out, the pain caused by having her hair dragged out with it was evident in her countenance.

The mother's life was ended. How I grieved to see that young lady, looking in her white dress even younger than she really was, sweet and gentle as a little lamb, led to the slaughter. I felt as though I were present at the martyrdom of one of those holy young virgins represented in the pictures of the great masters.

The same thing which occurred in her mother's case happened in hers,—the same oversight as to the pin, the same pain, the same calm, the same death! How the red blood flowed down from her head and her throat!

'Now she is happy!' I cried to myself as I saw her body thrown into the horrible coffin.

May the all-powerful and all-merciful God grant to their family every blessing they may desire, and that I ask for my own, and bring us all together with those who have gone before into that abode where there is no more Revolution, into that country which shall have, as Saint Augustine says,—

'Truth for its King,

Charity for its Law,

And Eternity for its Duration'.

---

14.   This friend whom Father Carrichon met was Father Brun, Priest of the Oratory, jointly with whom I had charge, at Juilly, of the Hall of the *Minimes* (the youngest pupils of the College), among whom were Messieurs Alexis and Alfred de Noailles. I had informed Monsieur Brun on the same day as Monsieur Carrichon (July 22, 1794) of our anxieties and our desires for Mesdames de Noailles. These two friends met in the Rue de Faubourg St. Antoine, accompanied the victims, gave them their blessing, and did not withdraw until after the completion of the final sacrifice.—*Note by Monsieur Grelet.*

LETTER FROM MADAME LA DUCHESSE DE DURAS, Née NOAILLES, TO MONSIEUR GRELET.

Be of good courage and He shall strengthen your heart,

all ye that hope in the Lord.—Ps. xxxi. 24.

How much you need to apply these sacred words to yourself in the trying situation in which Providence has placed you! We have already tested your courage in a most wonderful way; it will not fail you, because it rests on the law of God, and in him alone you have put your trust. What would the father and mother of these unfortunate children feel if you should abandon them? But what am I saying? They will deserve the continuation of your tender cares on account of their sweetness and perfect obedience. I love to believe that they will inherit some of the virtues of the angel whom we mourn. That lovely mother opened her pure heart to you; you should inculcate in her children all that she valued, all that she felt. She regarded you as their brother, and treated you as such. It is as a sister, and also one who shared her confidence, that I am now speaking to you; for I am not sure of having an opportunity of telling you with my lips all I think. If Heaven spares my life it will be a precious moment to me (who could imagine one more so?) when I find myself once more with you and them, talking together of our dear lost ones, and encouraging one another to profit by their admirable examples. We will say to them, 'Be Christians and you will be faithful to every duty; study human sciences, because they will help you to be useful to humanity; but above all, and before everything else, be good.'

I think it is necessary that they should know perfectly well how to calculate, etc.

I have given up everything; I have ceased to think of anything earthly, and keep my mind fixed upon heaven. I must close. I am, perhaps, speaking to you for the last time. I know not what Providence has in store for me; but whatever it may be I shall never cease to remember the debt I owe you, which can only be equalled by my confidence in you.

EXTRACT FROM THE 'MÉMORIAL EUROPÉEN,' APRIL 24, 1809.

Near the old village of Picpus, now a part of the Faubourg St. Antoine, under the walls of the garden which belonged to the canoness of St. Augustine, in a bit of ground not more than thirty feet in length, repose thirteen hundred and fifteen victims beheaded at the Barrière du Throne between the 26th Prairial and the 9th Thermidor in the second year of the Republic.

Widows, orphans, and mothers left comfortless, and without support, swallowed their tears in secret, and dared not even ask for their dead the right of burial. In times like those, tears had ceased to be innocent, and the tomb to be a refuge. These unhappy creatures contented themselves with commending the remains of their loved ones to Him whose eye is ever upon the living and the dead; but they knew not whose hand buried them, nor even the spot of earth where they were laid.

But a Sister as brave as she was tender, Madame Amélie-Zéphirine de Salm-Kirbourg, Princess of Hohenzollern, sister of Frédérick, Prince of Salm, gained from her great grief a strength which others seemed to lose. She had, I may say, watched over the last moments of her brother's life, had seen the blow which ended his days, the wagon which bore away his remains, the earth which received them. She bought the spot of ground, scarcely sufficient to cover the victims who had just been buried there; she had it enclosed by a wall, and she protected it from profanation, hoping that pious sorrow would some day consecrate these new catacombs. This prayer of fraternal piety has been heard; it has been fulfilled by two sisters, Mesdames de la Fayette and de Montagu, worthy imitators of such an example, for they were themselves worthy of setting it. They both belonged to one of those patrician families which had remained sound in the midst of an age despoiled of virtue, like an obelisk in the midst of a desert; both were daughters, granddaughters, sisters, and were related to and nearly connected with several victims beheaded at the Barrière du Throne. One of them, whose days were fewer than her good works, died last year, leaving in the world, in which she has lived only to be wife and mother, a void difficult to fill; the other, with a broken heart, a worn-out body, and her fortune all lost, still finds comfort for the sorrowful, solace for the suffering, and help for the poor. These two noble and pious women began by purchasing a portion of the ground belonging to the nuns; and upon the ruins of the cells they have caused to be built a modest oratory. The innocence of the former occupants must help to make effectual the prayers to be offered there. The august symbol of our redemption has now been placed above this funeral enclosure; a priest has been sent there by the Grand Vicars of Paris; an annual service has been appointed there; and the blood of a Divine Victim has been offered upon this altar for the repose of the souls of all these distinguished dead.

This was doubtless sufficient for the dignity and consolation of all these Christian spirits, but not to satisfy the tender pity of their families and friends. The chapel and the cemetery were separated from each other by the garden of the nuns. It was resolved to unite them by purchasing this valuable bit of ground, which contains more than four *arpents*. A subscription was started. A circular was drawn up by a man noted for talent and integrity,[15] who for thirty years has declared himself the defender of all those whose misfortunes were most noble and touching. Generous emotion responded to the appeal of eloquent sensibility, and subscriptions were soon obtained to the amount of forty thousand francs. By the side of the proudest and most cherished names of France one cannot see without emotion the unknown names and small donations of several faithful servants who brought their humble offerings to lay at the feet of their old masters and at the base of the new altar. The whole of the piece of ground was at last purchased; and for two years and a half the same enclosure has surrounded the victims and the oratory of the dead. The ashes of the fathers have become the property of the children; the children will transmit it to their descendants. This monument will remain as a sorrowful reparation for the past and an impressive lesson to the future.

Here every day the holy sacrifice is offered up for all the victims of the Revolution; here are celebrated every year for those buried in this spot two solemn services,—one on Low Sunday week and the other on the day corresponding to the 9th Thermidor; here on last Monday, the 11th of this month, a congregation gathered to celebrate the anniversary. After the service at the chapel, which was remarkable only for the number and emotion of those present, the attendants went in procession, according to custom, into the Champ des Martyrs.

In the middle there is a bit of rising ground shaded by cypress and poplar trees, whose tall waving branches remind us of the vanity of our earthly hopes, and point to where they should be fixed; while a cross surmounting a pyramid, whose base is planted upon all these vanished sources of happiness, seems to call all the descendants of the victims to its outstretched arms. The funeral memorial service began, and the faithful, on their knees, alternately repeated the melancholy stanzas of the psalm which mourns and hopes.

———

<u>15</u>. Monsieur Lally-Tollendal.

9 789362 519733